GAMES TEACHERS MAKE

by Joyce Gallagher

Incentive Publications, Inc.
Nashville, Tennessee

Cover and illustrations by Kathleen Bullock
Edited by Sherri Y. Lewis

ISBN 0-86530-210-3

Table Of Contents

Games, Ideas, And Inspirations

INTRODUCTION

If you've been looking for ways to incorporate your game ideas, GAMES TEACHERS MAKE may be the answer!

Now your good ideas need no longer grow stale! This book tells you how to make a game board – how big it should be, how to make it sturdy, how to incorporate your idea, and plenty of helpful hints to make your game boards last.

"How do I keep pockets from tearing on game boards?" Use naugahyde pockets, of course!

"But I can't draw. How can I make a nice-looking game board?" Try using colorful wallpaper squares from wallpaper sample books!

These suggestions, a materials-needed list, and more plus step-by-step instructions on game board ideas and reproducible patterns are included. Each game/game board idea is preceded by a grade level, purpose of the game and what can be learned by students, materials needed to make and play the game, instructions and rules, and variations to try when students master the original version.

This "how-to" instruction book makes cutting and pasting fun and helps you develop and use gamesmanship and game boards to the fullest. Your final products should provide learning fun and excitement for you and your students for years to come.

Getting It All Together

Materials to have on hand

Careful reading of this section will provide hints and tips for creating the materials illustrated in this book.

POSTER BOARD – Available in white and other colors. Stiff poster, 6-ply, is the best weight for the game board. Semistiff, 4-ply, should be used for shaped items such as outlines of states that must be cut out by hand. Using poster board colored on both sides allows double use of the poster with a different game on each side.

GAME CARDS – Use a paper cutter to cut scrap poster board into 2" x 4" pieces. Store in a shoe box for a ready supply when game cards are needed.

FILE FOLDERS – Available in manila or colors. Use a sturdy weight (11-point) for durability.

FILE JACKETS – File folders with closed ends. Use for picture file.

CONSTRUCTION PAPER – Choose an 80 pound basis weight for a durable paper that is bright and will fold without cracking. Useful for making task cards, game board decorations, answer keys, or even game cards.

GUMMED ART PAPER – Available at art and educational supply stores. Cut out shapes, lick, and stick. Useful in making game tracks (see page 14) or for decorating game boards and file folder activities.

PICTURES – For decorating teacher-made activities and even for making the game track. Create a ready supply by making a picture file. (See page 18.)

CARDBOARD PIECES – In varying sizes for making flip charts illustrated on pages 68-70.

INDEX CARDS – Lined and unlined, index cards are available in a variety of sizes and colors. The 5" x 8" size is ideal for making task cards and answer keys. Cards can also be cut into 1" x 5" strip tags as illustrated with games on page 25.

SELF-ADHESIVE PAPER – In solids or patterns for covering small storage boxes which will hold game cards and board markers. Cut leftover scraps into freehand shapes for game tracks (see page 16.)

CARBON PAPER, TISSUE PAPER, ONION SKIN PAPER – For tracing patterns onto poster board or folders.

CLEAR PACKAGING TAPE – Useful for reinforcing hole-punched areas or high-stress points.

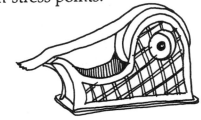

COLORED ADHESIVE DOTS – In a variety of shapes, sizes, and colors to make quick-and-easy game tracks (see pages 14-17).

VELCRO DOTS – Available in craft or sewing shops, are useful where students must match and attach answers.

MAGNETIC TAPE – Available in craft shops in long strips which can be cut to size needed. Use in ways similar to velcro dots.

CRAFT GLUE – Several good brands are available in craft shops. When gluing velcro or magnetic tape to laminated surfaces, place a dot of glue on back of velcro and a dot of glue on the laminated surface to give a permanent bond. Do not store glued items in extreme heat.

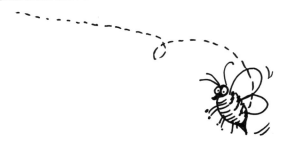

HOT GLUE GUN – Will create an excellent bond when attaching velcro or magnetic tape to laminated surfaces.

MARKERS – Permanent and watercolor. Permanent markers are bright and will not fade quickly – best for outlining and lettering. However, they will more readily bleed through to the back of the paper surface. Watercolor markers are available in a greater variety of colors and provide softer shades.

COLORED PENCILS – Provide soft colors in a great variety and they laminate nicely.

BRADS – Use 1" brads with small to medium heads.

FLATHEAD STOVE BOLTS – Are used in

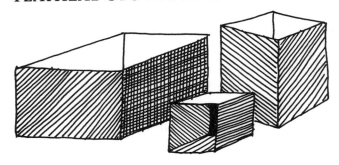

making spinners (see page 35). Best size is 1/2" x 3/16" available in hardware stores.

SMALL STURDY BOXES – Such as jewelry, stationery, or checkbook boxes, for storing game pieces and cards. Bottoms of cheese boxes covered with self-adhesive paper are great for classroom display of a stack of 5" x 8" task cards.

MEDIUM-SIZED MARGARINE TUBS – Use unmarked containers with tight-fitting lids for spinner and storage all in one.

METAL RINGS – The kind that open like a key ring, available at office supply stores in various sizes. Use for hanging cards, flip charts, folding game boards (see pages 68-70), etc.

SCRAPS OF NAUGAHYDE (LEATHER-LIKE FABRIC) – Check at upholstery shops, auto seat cover shops, and remnant counters at fabric shops. There is nothing better than naugahyde for making pockets on game boards (see page 24). If naugahyde is unavailable, vinyl wallpaper samples will do. Naugahyde is stretchy and can be wiped clean. It is attached **after** the game board is laminated and can be placed anywhere on the board if a long-reach stapler is used.

LONG-REACH STAPLER – Expensive, but so useful in attaching naugahyde pockets and stapling reading materials into file folders that it is well worth the expense. Perhaps the school PTA will purchase one. Several teachers might join together to get one. Or, why not ask for one for Christmas?

STENCILS FOR LETTERING – Many kinds are available. Try to find a brand with various sizes (2", 4", and 5" are good to have).

GAME MARKERS – For movement around the game board, can be salvaged from old games (check at garage sales). Tiny toys can be purchased at toy and party supply stores.

LAMINATING FILM – Use **matte** film for a dull, satin finish or **gloss** film for a shiny finish. Available in rolls 200' x 22".

DRY MOUNT TISSUE – Use with laminating films for uniform adhesion. Comes in rolls or in boxes of 500 sheets (8" x 11" or 9" x 12").

SCISSORS

X-ACTO® KNIFE

HOLE PUNCH – Some office supply stores now have a small, single-hole drill punch for use in punching holes that are wanted in places other than along the edge of a poster or file folder.

SCRAPS OF KNITTING YARN

RUBBER CEMENT

RUBBER CEMENT THINNER

RULER

YARDSTICK

T-STICK

Note: For each game described in this book, there is a list of materials needed. The list will include sizes and colors but will not specify scissors, rubber cement, markers, rulers, or laminating film since those things will be used for almost all items constructed.

The Main Event
Creating a snazzy, jazzy game board

Size • Theme • Pictures • Game Track • Lettering • Pockets

How Big Should The Game Board Be?

The size of an uncut poster board (22" x 28") often dictates the size of the game board, but there are several advantages to making game boards that are slightly smaller. An ideal size is 18" x 20" which will fit better on student desks, is more easily stored, and best of all, will fit into a seal-press type laminating machine in one step.

When a larger game board is desired, lamination and storage can be made easier by the creation of a fold-up game board. Cut a full-size poster board in half, design the board, and laminate each half separately. Punch matching holes and put the two halves together with metal rings or pieces of yarn.

Hint: Cutting the board in half **first** allows the game track to be designed so that no track segment straddles the center cut.

What Theme Will This Game Have?

At a "Make-it, Take it" workshop, the leader stopped beside a teacher who was putting the final touches on a game board entitled, "What Do You Know About the Civil War?"

"It's neat and colorful," complimented the instructor, "but why have you decorated a game board for a Civil War unit with space ships and astronauts?"

"To make it appealing for my fifth-grade boys," was the reply. Then the teacher solved his own problem, "I guess I should have used pictures of the Monitor and the Merrimac...or cannons..." Then he observed, "It doesn't hang together very well, does it?"

It must "hang together." That says it all. Pictures, decorations, color, and title should all come together to create a total theme.

Theme will be suggested by several things:

1. The content or skill to which the activity relates.

2. Related pictures you have found that say, "These would look neat on a game board."

3. The interests and ages of the students who will use the game.

I. Content-oriented games are easiest to design. Use pictures, colors, and game title suited to content being reviewed.

EXAMPLES

A. To review a unit on "Our State," use pictures of the state symbols (flag, bird, tree, flower). Use colors that appear in the state flag. Put a picture of the capitol building in the winner's spot and title the game, "Reach the Capitol."

B. Decorate a game to review and reinforce multiplication facts with large cutout numbers with comic faces, the "times" sign, and the title, "Oh, my! Multiply!"

C. Small animals cut from old workbooks can march across a game on animals identification. A good title, "Visit the Zoo."

D. A unit of study on Indians lends itself to a review game board splashed with Indians and tepees (try wallpaper). A tepee makes a good winner's spot with the title, "Reach the Tepee."

II. Skill-related games can be livened up with any bright pictures suitable to the age of those using the activity. Be sure pictures are related and game title fits the pictures used.

EXAMPLES

A. Use honey bees to decorate a game called, "Bee Wise."

B. To provide practice in recognizing and using homonyms, sprinkle a board with "happy faces" (stickers or cut from wallpaper) and call it "Happy-Face Homonyms."

Hint: Alliteration using the same first letter for each major word in a title makes a snappy game name.

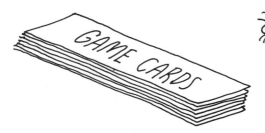

III. Consider ages and interests of students who will use the game. Teddy bears are obviously not the best choice for sixth graders (unless, of course, the game is about the life and times of Teddy Roosevelt). Find out what your students' interests are by listening! What do they talk about on the playground? In the lunch line? During sharing time?

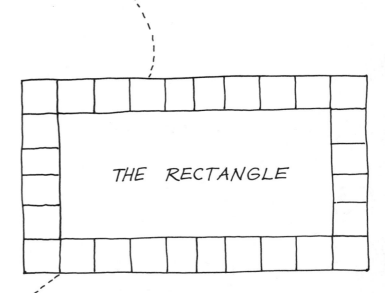

MAKING TRACKS

When someone says, "game track," do you immediately think of a straight, evenly spaced track around the edge of a board?

It takes a long time to measure and draw all those exactly-the-same-size squares, doesn't it?

TRY THIS TIMESAVER

On sheets of lightweight (for ease in cutting) poster board about 18" x 20", measure and draw several game tracks in a variety of shapes as illustrated below.

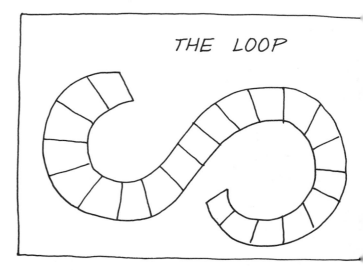

THE BACKWARD 'S"

THE COIL

THE SQUARE COIL

Cut out each track. Laminate and trim closely and you have patterns to make five different game tracks without having to measure every time. Just lay the track on poster board and trace around it putting a dot on either side of the track where each line segment comes to the edge. Remove the pattern and use a ruler to connect dots. Outline the track with colored marker. Decorate the area around the game track with suitable pictures and an appropriate title. Instant game board (maybe not "instant," but quick)!

MORE QUICK TRICKS WITH GAME TRACKS

1. Why not make a **SPOT TRACK** by cutting freehand spots from lick-and-stick art paper or from scraps of self-adhesive paper. Stick them on poster board in a track pattern. Use a marker to connect the spots with squiggly lines.

2. Nothing's quicker than a **STICKER!** Since sticker-collecting became popular, the variety is endless. There are stickers to scratch-and-sniff and stickers to pinch-and-squeeze. There are glow-in-the-dark stickers and message stickers. Some are padded and puffy. Others are furry and fuzzy. Of course, there are still stickers of the plain variety – just cute and colorful.

Why not make a quicky-sticker game board? All you need is a batch of stickers, a good picture for the winner's spot, a marker, and a piece of poster board. Glue the picture in the lower right corner. Arrange the stickers in an interesting pattern progressing from upper left to the winner's spot. Leave room for a title and a 2" x 4" rectangle in which to place game cards. Connect stickers with marker lines. Letter the title. Laminate. Presto! A game board!

16

3. ADHESIVE DOTS can be found in a variety of geometric shapes and colors. Use dots and bright pictures for a "make-tonight, use-tomorrow" game board.

4. Combine **DOTS** and **STICKERS**. Use dots for the game track, and group a batch of stickers in one corner for the winner's spot, or use stickers as decoration.

5. WALLPAPER patterns can inspire ideas for game boards. A wallpaper sample that was an arrangement of various sizes of yellow bricks interspersed with yellow flowers led to the creation of a game board entitled, "Follow the Yellow Brick Road." Bricks were cut out and arranged in a road pattern with bricks slightly touching or overlapping each other at various

angles. Flowers were gathered in one corner for the winner's spot and labeled, "Golden Flower Patch." A 2" x 4" game card rectangle and a few minutes at the laminating machine completed a board to be used with any set of cards and any grade level.

6. Try a **POSTER** game board! Every teacher accumulates large posters which are used on bulletin boards as decoration or to spark discussion. Why not mount a large poster on a poster board background (for stability) and make a game track around the edge with a trail of stars or other stickers? The poster can still be used on the bulletin board and can double as a game board. Do this with several posters and you have enough game boards to divide the class into groups with a game for each!

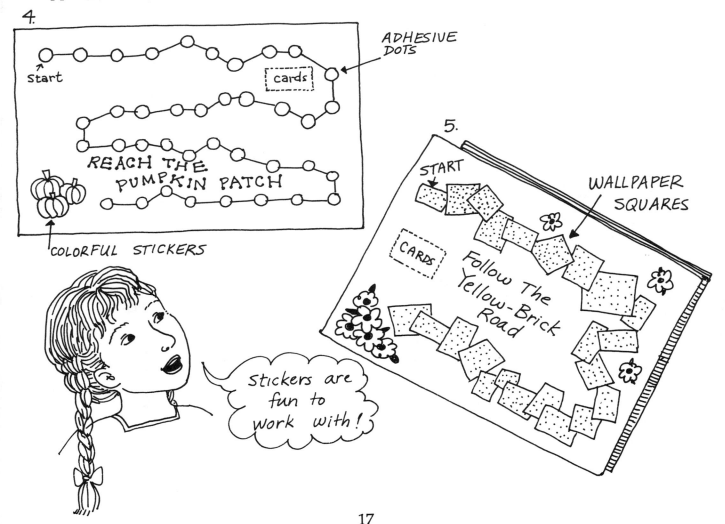

WHERE DO YOU GET ALL THOSE CUTE PICTURES?

This was a question asked of a workshop instructor who had scores of games and activities on display. Everything she had seemed to be decorated with just the right picture – games, file folders, task cards. In answer to the question, she went to one end of a long table and laid her hand on a self-adhesive covered cardboard box the size of a large breadbox.

"This," she said, "is my picture file."

The box was filled with file jackets (closed end file folders) that were stuffed with pictures from every source imaginable. Folder labels ranged from "Animals" to "Yellow." There was a folder for each month of the year and one for each significant holiday. Each basic color had a folder as did each school subject. Charlie Brown peeked from a folder labeled, "Cartoon Characters." A leafy oak grew from one marked, "Trees." One folder boasted, "Happy Faces," another lamented, "Sad Faces." One well-worn folder was labeled, "Lettering" and held samples of letters and writing.

The fattest folder of all bulged with pictures of pretty borders, colorful and unusually shaped arrows and question marks, eye-catchers – items that could not categorize into other folders but could be used to say **anything**. This ballooning folder was labeled, "Attention-Getters."

The workshop instructor explained that she saw every magazine or newspaper, advertisement, or package as a potential source of material for the picture file. She simply ripped or clipped and added to the appropriate folder.

"And now," she concluded, "when I need **just the right picture**, I don't have to waste time searching. I can almost always find what I need in my picture file."

Having pictures on hand is the perfect answer for the most-often expressed complaint heard at teacher workshops, "I can't draw!"

Lucky is the teacher who is talented enough to draw pictures and decorations on game boards. But for teachers who are not artistic enough to do this – **START A PICTURE FILE!**

Pictures, Pictures Everywhere!

Sources of Pictures

1. WALLPAPER SAMPLE BOOKS – Possibly the best source of large, brightly colored, virtually fadeless pictures.

Wallpaper samples often have half-pictures that are right at the edge of the paper. Don't throw these away. Glue about 1/8" from the edge of the game board to get an interesting effect, for example, a car just "driving onto the scene."

2. OLD WORKBOOKS – Provide scores of small, colorful pictures – an ideal size for use on game tracks and task cards.

3. TEXTBOOKS – SAMPLES OR READY-FOR-DISCARD. Does your bookshelf contain publisher's samples unused for years because you "can't cut up a book"? Cut it up! Not only for the pictures but for extra-time reading materials as well.

4. MAGAZINES – Some of the most unusual and brightest pictures to be found are in advertisements. Use children's magazines for pictures and ideas for games, activities, reading material.

5. TRAVEL/TOURISM BROCHURES AND POSTERS – Small pictures on travel brochures are useful for games and file folders to use when teaching about countries, states, cities, and geographical regions. Large posters make great game boards. (See page 12.)

6. CATALOGS – Especially those from education suppliers and publishing houses are full of tiny illustrations. Some catalogs have an illustration theme with recurring pictures. One teacher decorated an entire game with small cutouts of Donald Duck clipped throughout a catalog.

7. BILLBOARD PAPER – Available in short end rolls from companies who do large-sign advertising. It is easy to cut and is fadeless. Try it for decorative cutouts.

8. WRAPPING PAPER – Not just flowers and stripes but colorful pictures suitable for all ages. Select the heavier weight paper, wrap your gift, and use the leftovers for...(See "Reach The Star" on page 108).

9. OUTDATED CALENDARS – Contain colorful drawings and pictures. Why not use one or more calendar pages as a game board? The squares are already there!

12. NEWSPAPERS – Appealing cartoon-type drawings often appear in ads. One teacher who could "not draw **anything**" even added a picture of a flowing ribbon to her pictures and then traced it onto several activities.

13. PACKAGING: SACKS/BOXES – Look for borders and symbols as well as pictures.

14. STICKERS – Are not just for rewarding work well-done! Use a pattern of stickers for a game track or to decorate a game board, folder, task card.

10. GREETING CARDS – Use a large one in the center of a poster board and design the game track around it, picking up the colors used on the card. Cartoon cards are great!

11. JUNK MAIL – Will add so much to your picture file that you will regret all the times you have thrown this stuff away without opening it.

HINT:

Do **not** use photographs to decorate materials that will be laminated. The heat may react with the chemicals in the photographic paper to turn it black or crack it. Some teachers have said they have laminated photos if the heat on the machine is low enough, but it's risky – you may lose the pictures.

From Picture File To Game Board

Now that you have a file bulging with pictures, how do you get them from file to game board?

1. If the picture is the right size, simply trim and glue.

2. If you don't want to glue the picture on (perhaps you want to save it for later use on something else or perhaps the color is wrong) then trace the picture to your poster board. Place the picture in the selected spot on the poster board, and put a sheet of carbon paper between picture and poster board. Using a pencil, trace the picture onto the board. Remove the original and the carbon and use a felt-tip marker to "draw" the picture (see the illustration below).

NOTE: Always work so your arm will rest only on lines completed with marker that has dried. Carbon lines will smudge.

3. Enlarge a tiny picture by using an opaque projector. Hang poster on a bulletin board, project the image onto the poster, and trace.

4. Another possibility – use a copy machine to make a duplicate of the picture, color, cut out, and glue onto the game board.

POSTER BOARD

CARBON PAPER

PICTURE TO TRACE

Be careful of carbon lines — they smudge!

But I Don't Do Letters!

Next to, "I can't draw," the most common complaint heard at make-it workshops is, "I can't letter."

It is true that the least attractive part of a teacher-made game is usually the lettering. Poor lettering and bad arrangement of letters can ruin an otherwise beautiful piece of work.

SEVERAL KINDS OF LETTERING HELPS CAN BE PURCHASED

1. Stencils come in a large variety of sizes and styles. An excellent choice is TRACING LETTERS (see materials list on page 10) which comes with several styles of punch-out letters in one box.

Be sure to keep the various styles separate as you punch in order to avoid a mixup.

2. Rub-on letters also come in a variety of styles and sizes, but the "rub-on" doesn't always transfer satisfactorily and must be filled in with black marker. These letters are expensive.

3. Peel-and-stick letters work well but are also expensive.

Why not be adventurous? Try some freehand lettering. The big advantage is that you can make the letters just the size you need to fit the space available. Spend some time practicing using the tips and tricks below, and soon you will wonder why you thought you could never do letters.

TIPS AND TRICKS FOR GOOD

FREEHAND LETTERING

1. Print. Printed letters always look better on a game board than written ones.

2. Take some time to measure. Leave about the same amount of space for each letter. Pencil in the measuring lines very lightly.

3. Pencil in the letters very lightly. Don't start with marker and just hope that it will all come out right.

4. Outline penciled-in letters with a fine-tip black marker. Fill in letters with colored marker of your choice.

5. If broad-tipped marker is used to draw letters, there may be ragged points on each letter. These can be squared and filled in carefully with a fine-tip marker.

6. Don't try to make all letters exactly straight and even. It's almost impossible. Avoid the problem by putting letters at various angles as in this illustration:

8. After letters have been outlined and colored with marker, wait until they are **completely dry**. Then erase all pencil marks before laminating.

When erasing pencil marks on games, use an art gum eraser which does not leave behind eraser crumbs like a pencil eraser. Those little crumbs can get caught under laminating film and leave noticeable flaws in the final product.

9. Be sure to collect various styles of lettering as you build your picture file. When you are ready for letters on a game board, go to the picture file and choose a style that will fit your game. Practice a little and then use them on your game.

7. Straight-line letters such as those above can be dressed up by adding a tiny perpendicular line or a tiny bulb at the end of each tip on the letter as illustrated.

You can do your own lettering. Don't "bee" afraid to try!

If Only The Pockets Would Last As Long As The Rest Of The Game!

Have you quit trying to make games and file folder activities that require pockets? Many teachers have because they find it so difficult to make pockets that will not tear or come loose soon after students begin to use the activity.

Don't give up! There is a way!

Nothing works better than a scrap of naugahyde (leather-like fabric) for making pockets. It's stretchy! It's washable! It won't tear! It can be cut into squares for conventional-type pockets or into shapes for unusual pockets.

This miracle fabric is available from upholstery shops or auto seat cover places (which may let you go through their scrap barrels at no charge). Fabric stores sell naugahyde, too. Don't forget to check the remnant table for bolt end-pieces.

In the unlikely event that naugahyde cannot be found, a second best choice is vinyl wallpaper found in sample books. Use the kind with thread-woven backing for extra sturdiness.

There is one catch! A naugahyde pocket must be stapled on rather than glued (but that's what makes it stay on so well). Stapling the pocket to the game board will require use of the long-reach stapler suggested in the materials list at the beginning of this book.

To attach the naugahyde pocket to the game board, follow these steps:

1. Be sure to leave sufficient room for the pocket. Allow blank space above the pocket so that question strips or word tags protruding from the pocket will not obscure any part of the game.

2. Cut naugahyde to size and shape desired. (See "Witch's Shoes" on page 104.)

3. Complete the rest of the game and LAMINATE BEFORE ATTACHING POCKET.

4. Position the pocket in selected spot on the laminated board and staple along sides and bottom.

Hint: When using a naugahyde pocket on a file folder, open the folder and attach pocket to the **right** side so that backs of the staples will appear only on the back of the folder and will not mar the decorated front side.

GAME BOARD

Start

POCKET

FINISH

Nifty!

Deal Out The Cards!

Timesaving tips for making game cards

1. On games where players will use a stack of cards, draw a 2" x 4" rectangle to hold game cards. Using same-size cards for all games is a timesaver.

This does not apply to games like Bingo and Concentration where many cards have to be laid side by side or games such as "Map Words" on page 75 in which strip tags are used.

2. Keep a ready supply of game cards on hand by cutting scrap poster board into 2" x 4" rectangles. Use a paper cutter to get neat, straight edges. Store ready-cut cards in a shoe box for easy access.

3. When you don't have ready-cut cards on hand, draw a grid of 2" x 4" rectangles on an 18" x 20" poster board. Print a word, a question, a problem, etc., in each rectangle. LAMINATE the finished board and THEN CUT into individual cards. This saves cutting twice.

4. Use colors for game cards to put "umph" in the game.

5. IMPORTANT: When making several stacks of cards that will be used with one generic game board, make each stack of cards a different color. It saves sorting!

6. Always PRINT information on cards.

7. When printing words, problems, or questions on cards, keep in mind the ages of the students who will use the cards and use appropriate vocabulary. Whatever the age, keep wording brief, simple, concise.

8. Spark up a set of game cards by decorating the back of each card in some small way. It doesn't need to be fancy – perhaps a colorful stripe across the card or a sticker. Or perhaps you have saved a set of thirty old workbooks and the same dog appears on page 25 of each book. Thirty dogs will decorate a big stack of cards!

STRIP TAGS

Some games will have words or problems on narrow tags which will be taken from or inserted into pockets. (See page 24.) Unlined index cards, 5" x 8", are perfect for making strip tags. With the card in a vertical position, line off eight 1 inch segments as illustrated below. Print a game item on each segment. LAMINATE and THEN CUT into strips.

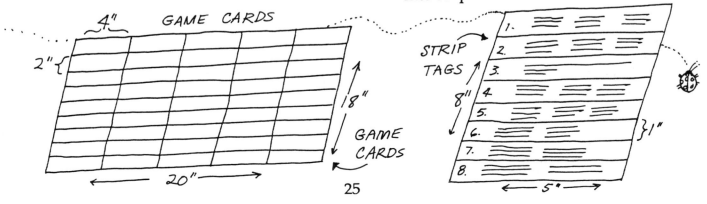

GAME CARDS IN SHAPES

Game cards need not always be rectangular. Use sturdy, colorful construction paper to cut shaped game cards. It takes longer, but it adds variety and spark to your creations.

Game Cards In Shapes

Game Cards Can Do More Than Just State The Problem!

1. Neither spinner nor dice is needed if you use the game card to tell players how many spaces to move forward after a correct answer. In the lower right corner of the game card, print in small letters "Move Ahead 1" if the question is an easy one. Use "Move Ahead 2" for questions of medium difficulty, and "Move Ahead 3" for hard questions. Of course, this instruction is disregarded and the player does not move at all if an incorrect answer is given.

2. One way to make a game self-checking is to put the correct answer on the **back** of each game card. Game cards should be laid **faceup** on the board. Make a cover card for the deck as illustrated below so that players cannot read cards ahead. The player will remove the cover card, take a question card and **lay it flat on the table** in front of him, taking care not to turn it over. The cover card is put back in place to cover the next question. After the player gives his/her answer, he/she turns the card over, reads aloud the correct answer, and moves accordingly. Instruction as to the number of spaces to move ahead should be printed beneath the correct answer.

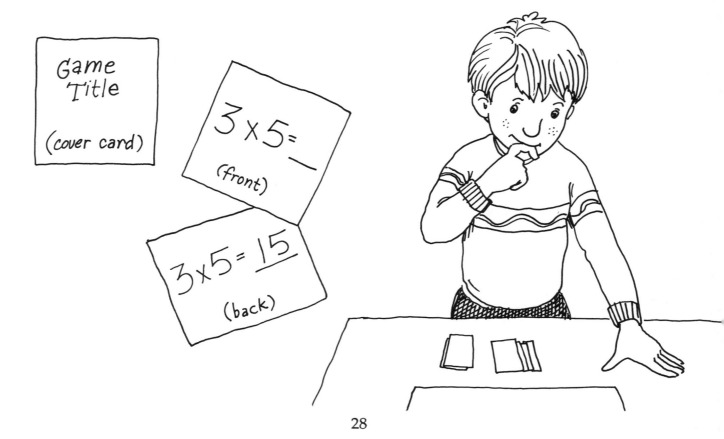

Game Title (cover card)

3 x 5 = ___ (front)

3 x 5 = 15 (back)

Penalty/ Reward Cards

Make your game more exciting by adding some penalty/reward cards to the deck. These should be the same color as the rest of the cards and interspersed throughout the deck so that players will draw them by chance.

EXAMPLE

"LET'S TRAVEL," a game in which players move tiny plastic cars along a "road" track could have the following penalties and rewards:

1. You blew a tire! Lose one turn.

2. You are a careful driver! Take an extra turn.

3. Good for you! You used your turn signals! Move ahead one space.

4. You ran out of gas? Go back to the gas station (placed near the beginning of the game).

5. You passed on a curve! How dangerous! Go back to START.

6. Engine trouble? Go back 3 spaces.

7. You obeyed the speed limit. Exchange places with the person just ahead of you or move ahead 3 spaces.

8. You threw trash out the car window. Lose a turn.

9. You took a parking spot that was marked "Handicapped" when you have no handicap. Go back 4 spaces.

Penalties and rewards should FIT THE THEME OF THE GAME.

NOTE: Penalty and reward cards can do some teaching on their own about right and wrong.

For primary children who have limited reading skills, penalty and reward statements should be kept very brief and simple:

1. Move 1 space.
2. Go back 2.
3. Lose 1 turn.
4. Go again.

Cards can be constructed that require no reading at all by using symbols that can be explained to players ahead of time.

Hint: Use the same symbols to mean the same things in all the games you construct. It makes it easier for children to remember the symbols and it avoids confusion.

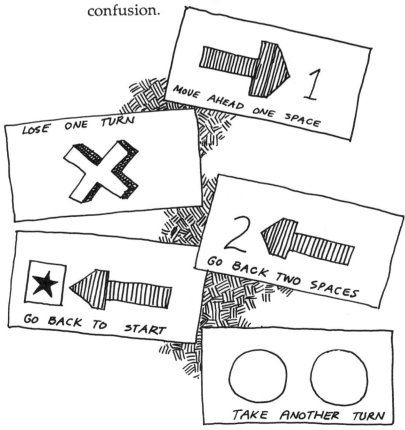

Alternate Ways To Add Penalties And Rewards To A Game

1. At random, choose several spots on the game track to be penalty/reward spots. Make these spots a color that will contrast with the rest of the game track or put an object on each spot such as a sticker or a star. When a player lands on a marked spot, he chooses a card from the penalty/reward deck. These cards should be a different color than the question cards and should be placed in a separate stack on the game board during play. Mark the back of each penalty/reward card in the same way that penalty/reward spots on the game board are marked.

Game rules should instruct: "Player landing on a spot with a star (or whatever) should choose a card from the blue stack and do what it says."

2. Penalties and rewards can also be inserted into a game by printing them directly on randomly chosen spots on the game track.

NOTE: This method does not allow for very many penalties and rewards, and once they are on the board, they cannot be varied.

Will It Work In The Classroom?

Establishing rules and procedures

Number of players • Who goes first • How to play • Ways to advance • Answer Keys

WHAT ARE THE RULES FOR THIS GAME?

In some ways, writing the rules and directions is the hardest part of creating a game. To make the job a little easier, keep these things in mind:

1. Type or print rules on a 5" x 8" index card. If the game has an answer key, put the rules on the reverse side. If a question arises about rules during the game, the judge can flip the answer key, refer to the rules, and answer the question.

2. Do not put the rules on the back of the game board since a need to read the rules would mean that all cards and playing pieces would have to be removed to turn the board over.

3. ALWAYS put the title of the game at the top of the rules card in case the card becomes separated from the game.

4. Decide on a format for stating rules and use that same format for all games. (See box on page 32.)

5. Number each step. This makes rules easier to follow in sequence. For younger students, present directions and rules in small steps.

6. Pictures and illustrations may be used to make directions more clear.

7. Using color and/or underlining may be used to call attention to the main words or phrases.

8. Be clear, concise, and explicit. State rules in SIMPLE LANGUAGE so that reading and understanding do not become problems. Listen to your students talk. Write rules and directions in similar sentences.

9. It is important that students know that this game is not being used just "for fun" but for a specific purpose. State the purpose clearly.

10. Unless it is very obvious, directions should be given for laying the game out.

11. Game procedures should be explained.

12. In all games, players should be instructed to always move to the left (clockwise). This establishes continuity and avoids confusion.

SUGGESTED FORMAT FOR RULES

Print the "Game Title"

1. State the purpose of the game.
2. Specify the number of players.
3. Unless it is very obvious, explain how to lay out the game.
4. Tell how to decide who will go first.
5. Explain the game procedure.
6. Tell what a player must do to win the game.

How Many Can Play This Game?

Written rules for a game should always specify the number of players. When deciding how many students should play, keep these things in mind:

1. Keep the number of players small – two, three, four at most.
   a. This allows play to move quickly, and players will not get impatient and restless between turns.
   b. Each player gets to answer more questions for increased practice and review.

2. For games that have answer keys, one extra participant is needed to be the JUDGE who will verify correct answers.
   a. Keep a record of who has served as the judge so that all students can be given an opportunity to perform this function.
   b. Watch out for the student who constantly volunteers to be judge in order to avoid the competition of the game.

3. Games that have pockets to be filled or emptied work best for two players who are competing against each other, but they may also be used for individual practice.

* Rules: REACH THE STAR

1. PURPOSE: Using antonyms and synonyms.
2. PLAYERS: 3 players and 1 Judge.
3. Place the game pieces on START
4. Player on the north side of the table goes first. Play moves to the left.
5. Take a card. Tell the Judge the card number.
6. Read the Question aloud. Answer aloud.
7. Judge reads the Answer aloud.
8. You're right? Move the number on the Question card.
9. Next player's turn.
10. Winner— first to reach the star!

* SAMPLE RULE CARD

Know the rules before you play the game!

WHO GOES FIRST?

When writing rules for games, use a variety of methods by which players can decide who goes first.

TRY THESE IDEAS:

1. Let the players themselves decide who will go first. This is good practice in decision-making and in learning to take turns.

2. The player with the longest (or shortest) first or last name goes first.

3. Players may alphabetize first (or last) names of all players. Player with first (or last) name closest to the beginning (or end) of the alphabet goes first.

4. The player facing the north, south, east, or west wall (specify one) goes first.

5. The judge will write a number from 1-10 on a scrap of paper. The player guessing closest to that number goes first.

6. The judge uses a scrap of paper for each player in the game. On one scrap

piece an "X" is printed. Players choose. The player who chooses the "X" goes first.

7. With the game pieces, include four buttons (for four players). All buttons are the same color except one. Players choose without looking. The player who chooses the odd color button goes first.

8. The player who is ready first (quietest) gets to go first. The judge may decide.

9. Of course, if the game uses dice or spinner, all players roll or spin. The one with the highest number goes first.

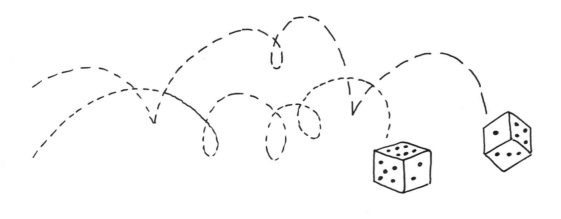

How Do I Get There From Here?

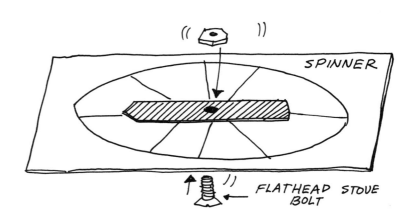

SPINNER

FLATHEAD STOVE BOLT

There are five ways to determine the number of spaces a player may advance around the game board when he/she gives a correct answer:

   a. Use a spinner.

   b. Use dice.

   c. State number of forward moves on game cards.

   d. State number of forward moves on answer key.

   e. Every answer yields a one-space forward move.

SPINNERS

Like pockets, teacher-made spinners are often unsatisfactory. Usually put together with a brad, they don't spin well. But there is a way to make a spinner that really works by using flathead stove bolts.

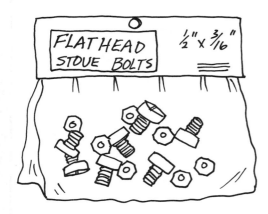

FLATHEAD STOVE BOLTS ½" x ³⁄₁₆"

MAKE A SPINNER THAT SPINS EVERY TIME

1. Cut a 9 inch square of heavy poster board.

2. Using a compass, draw a circle 8 inches in diameter in the center of the square.

3. Mark the circle into six equal segments.

4. In three of the segments, print a large "1"; in two segments, print a large "2"; and in the last segment, print a large "3."

Hint: It is best to have only 1's, 2's, and 3's on a spinner. This gives each player more opportunities to answer questions by landing on more spaces, and it keeps the game from going too fast.

5. Cut a strip of poster board to a 1" x 4" size, and cut one end to an arrow point.

6. Laminate the spinner board and the arrow.

7. With a hole punch, punch a hole in the center of the arrow.

8. Using an ice pick, pencil, or other sharp object, make and enlarge a hole in the center of the spinner.

9. Thread a flathead stove bolt (1/2" x 3/16") from the bottom up through the center hole in the spinner. (BE SURE THE STOVE BOLT HAS A FLATHEAD.)

10. Drop the arrow on the bolt. Affix a nut to the bolt.

11. Loosen the nut for use. Tighten for storage.

b. Dice are noisy and are often rolled off the game board onto table or floor.
c. Dice are easily lost.

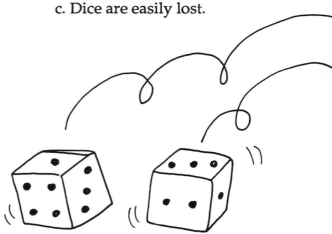

DICE

There are several disadvantages in using dice:

a. Dice are usually numbered up to six. When players roll four, five, or six, too many spaces are skipped over in one turn, and opportunities to answer questions are missed. In addition, the game moves too quickly.

STATE FORWARD MOVEMENT ON GAME CARD

This procedure is explained in the game cards section on pages 24-30.

STATE FORWARD MOVEMENT ON ANSWER KEY

a. At the end of each correct answer on the answer key, indicate in parentheses the number of forward spaces. (Move 1 space for easiest questions, 2 for questions of medium difficulty, and 3 for hardest questions.)
b. When the judge reads the correct answer, he/she will tell the player how many spaces to move forward.

EACH CORRECT ANSWER YIELDS A ONE-SPACE FORWARD MOVEMENT

This is the easiest way to move around the board, but it does not give any advantage to the player who correctly answers more difficult questions.

WHERE'S MY GAME PIECE?

Some games use spinners, some use dice. Some games use game cards, some have questions directly on the board. There can be variety in many aspects of a game board, but there is one CONSTANT – EVERY PLAYER MUST HAVE A GAME PIECE.

The simplest thing to do is to give each player a bean, a penny, or a button. But there is something about using beans or pennies that somehow detracts from the game. Remember how much it added to Monopoly® when you got to use the "Top Hat" or "Iron"? After going to all the trouble of making a really "spiffy" game, why stop now?

Visit a toy supply house or the plan-a-party section at a local variety store. All kinds of miniature objects can be found. These tiny treasures are often in packages of four or six; some are available individually for a few cents each.

Keep the theme of the game in mind when choosing game pieces. Use tiny plastic cars (each a different color) for a race-track game. Tiny flags go well with a game about America. Miniature shoes can "Walk Along" or "Track Down."

Check out the garage sales in your neighborhood. Old games can yield game markers and perhaps other usable pieces as well.

Put some imagination into it! Even buttons are available in novel shapes!

NOTE: When instructing younger students about use of games, be sure to include a few words of caution about putting game pieces in the mouth.

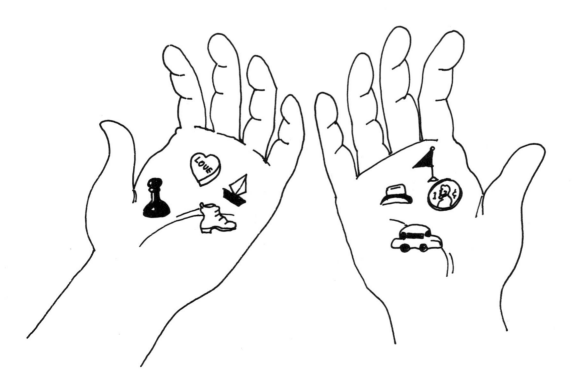

CHECK IT OUT!

In order to use a game without teacher supervision, players must have a way to check answers.

MAKE AN ANSWER KEY TO GO WITH EACH GAME

1. An index card (5" x 8") is stiff enough when laminated to provide long use but is flexible enough to be rolled into a typewriter for typing answers.

2. Heavy-weight construction paper can be used if color is desired to coordinate with the game. (Index cards also come in several pastel shades.)

3. ALWAYS put the name of the game at the top of each answer key in case it becomes separated from the game.

4. Be sure to number the items printed on game cards or game board. Then number the coordinating items on the answer key so the judge can find the correct answer.

5. Add a colorful touch to the answer key by decorating with a small picture to coincide with the theme of the game.

6. Since answer keys are small and may be lost, you can save replacement time by making two keys for each game. Alphabetize the extras according to game titles and store them in a safe place. If one of these must be added to a game, make another for the "backup box" to keep a ready supply of spares.

Instead of using an answer key, correct answers can be provided on the back of question cards as discussed on page 28.

To cut down on the number of game pieces to keep track of, put rules on one side of an index card and the answer key on the other side.

WHAT IF THERE ARE TOO MANY ANSWERS TO FIT ON AN INDEX CARD?

In the case of a game that has many cards, such as the "Your State" Game on page 99, use a file folder to provide an answer key. Type the answers, trim the pages, and glue them inside the file folder. Decorate the front of the folder with the game title and coordinating pictures.

A folded piece of colored construction paper will also provide a multisided answer key.

Use folded construction paper or a file folder.

Kid-Test It!

APPROVED

The game board is designed and decorated; cards are made and spinner is constructed; answer key is typed; rules are written out. Everything is ready to laminate. But wait!

Has your game been kid-tested? Have you worded the rules so that players will understand what to do? Can students figure out how to lay out and use the game? Even though you will explain new games as they are introduced, there will be times when students will use games for individual or small group activity and they will need to know how to proceed without repeated explanations.

Check it out! Give your newly-constructed game to a few selected students with instructions to "figure out how to play this."

Students who are "road-testing" a game will be sure to point out errors in spelling and lettering. (Don't kids love to catch teacher mistakes?) If the students need much help in deciding how to play the game, perhaps the rules need to be rewritten in clearer, simpler language.

Keep in mind that this is just a "road test" — a check to see if the game is understandable. When the time comes to begin using the game in the classroom, teacher explanation and introduction should always precede student use. Show the game, explain its purpose, and go through the rules of play step-by-step.

If students have not used any kind of game before, this would be the time for general instruction. Tell students where games will be stored and under what conditions they may be used. Emphasize care of materials and putting games away after use. You may wish to discuss some consequences for those who do not use and care for materials in an appropriate manner.

Don't Start Over! Fix It!

What if there are mistakes in the game? Do you just trash the whole thing? Never! Too much planning and hard work have gone into that game to quit now!

Most mistakes can be corrected!

1. Cover tiny mistakes with small pictures that fit the theme of the game.

2. A mistake in the game title can be corrected by covering the entire title with a strip of colored construction paper cut to fit, glued over the wrong title, and relettered. (See illustration below.)

3. Rule cards, game cards, and answer keys can simply be replaced.

4. It is not a good idea to try to correct lettering mistakes with liquid correction fluid. The ink often bleeds through the liquid or leaves a blob. Such corrections are enhanced under laminating film.

41

TURN ON THE LAMINATING MACHINE!

Do not for one minute be tempted to let students use a new game before it is laminated! No matter how careful they might be, a roomful of students cannot help but cause wear and tear. That wear and tear means hours of hard work down the drain.
LAMINATE BEFORE USING!

TIPS FOR SUCCESSFUL LAMINATING

1. There are two kinds of laminating film: gloss for a shiny finish and matte for a dull, satiny finish. Gloss gives a prettier finish, but when used where sunlight falls on the game, there can be a glare.

2. There are two kinds of laminating machines: seal-press and roll-type.
  a. The roll-type can handle larger items in one step, but time cannot be controlled, and edges are sometimes not secure which can result in peeling.
  b. Time and temperature are easily manipulated on the seal-press machine, although large items may have to be laminated in two steps which is tricky.

3. Wait until ink and glue are completely dry before laminating. Hasten drying by placing materials in a hot machine for a few seconds without film.

4. Laminating will **not** prevent fading. Do not leave materials on bookshelves or window ledges where they are exposed to direct sunlight. (Red and blue poster boards seem to be more susceptible to fading than other colors.)

5. If you are a first-time laminator, carefully read the instruction book that goes with your machine before you begin.

6. Keep **shiny side out** when wrapping items with film.

7. After wrapping the item in laminating film and before inserting it into the machine, trim away any sizable scraps. These can be used to laminate small items such as answer keys, rule cards, and game cards.

8. Place film-wrapped item inside a folded piece of brown craft paper to prevent exposed inside areas of film from sticking to the inside of the machine.

9. After lamination while the item is still hot, weight it with several heavy books to prevent curling.

10. Do not laminate two pieces of board or construction paper that are glued together edge to edge. They will peel apart. Cut one piece smaller than the other to leave a background edge to which the laminating film can adhere as illustrated below.

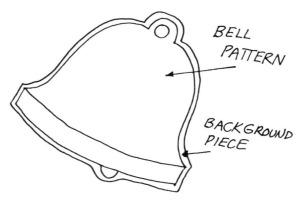

BELL PATTERN

BACKGROUND PIECE

11. Photographs do not laminate well. They may crack or turn black.

12. To laminate a deck of game cards, lay cards out on half a piece of laminating film. Fold top half of film over the cards. Use the small, long-handled "iron" that comes with the machine to iron the film onto the cards just enough to hold everything in place until it can be put into the machine. This will prevent cards or other small items from slipping and perhaps overlapping. If there is not an ironing tool with the machine, use an old household iron on medium-high heat. Do not use a good iron. If inside of film is accidentally touched with iron, a sticky residue will be left on the bottom of the iron.

13. When laminating large items that will not fit in the machine in one step, do not cover the entire piece with film at first. Covering the entire item with film and then "cooking" only half of it may cause moisture to gather under the end of the board not in the machine. This moisture may cause marker colors or even the dye in the board to run.

   To avoid this problem, cover only one half of the board with film; laminate; then cover the other half overlapping the already-laminated half about 1/8". Laminate this second half.

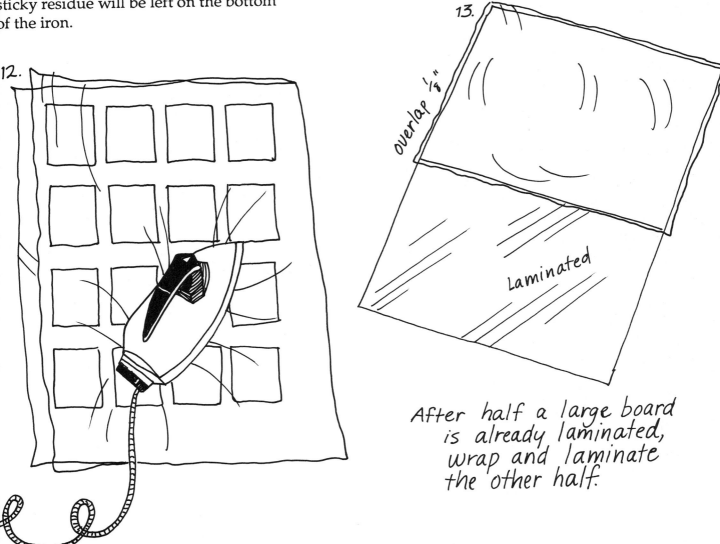

12.

13.

overlap 1/8"

Laminated

After half a large board is already laminated, wrap and laminate the other half.

43

The Flexible File Folder

QUESTIONS FOR YOU

Do you have NO storage space?

Do you have very little room for students to spread out with a game board?

Do you have a number of students who need individualized practice?

Do you have a wide variety of reading levels among your students?

YES? YES? YES? and YES?
Then try creating some file folder activities.

File folders require minimal storage space.

File folders can be used in small areas.

File folders are useful for single-student practice.

File folders can be used to present reading material above and below grade level.

HOWEVER...
CONSIDER THESE DISADVANTAGES

An open file folder will not lay as flat as a poster board game board.

The size of the file folder limits the use of game cards and other game pieces.

File folder games are not easy for students to group around.

Game pieces for folder activities are very small and more easily misplaced than large game pieces.

Try These Folder Ideas

1. COLORING BOOK GAME TRACK FOLDERS

Look on the coloring book stand at a variety store. Activity books, especially Halloween and Christmas, often have two-page game tracks that can be cut out, colored, and glued inside a file folder. Decorate the front of the folder with a greeting card or other appropriate picture from your picture file. Laminate.

These games have little content value but are helpful for teaching children to follow directions and to work together in groups.

Of course, you can create your own games for file folders. Some of the ideas in this book can be made on file folders rather than on poster board.

2. ONE-OF-A-KIND PICTURE FOLDERS

In an activity book or a children's magazine, you have found a brightly colored picture that could be used for practicing a skill such as visual discrimination. But you only have **one** picture! What to do? Cut out the picture and:

a. Use a colored folder that has two inside pockets. Decorate the front of the folder.

b. On the inside left pocket, print this instruction:

"Look at the picture in this pocket."

c. On the inside right pocket, print these instructions:

"Do the work sheet in this pocket."

"Check your paper with the answer key."

"Use only **one** work sheet."

d. Glue the selected picture to a piece of poster board.

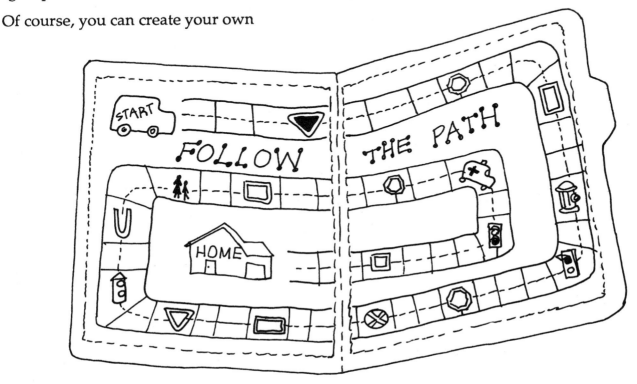

NOTE: Before using this folder, students should be instructed as to the importance of using only **one** work sheet: "Students, I have made enough work sheets for each student to have just **one**. Do not use a second one without asking me first."

ALTERNATE METHOD

a. Use a regular folder.

b. Glue the selected picture to inside left.

c. Glue one copy of the work sheet to inside right.

d. On the front of the folder, instruct students to:

"Open the folder."

"Look at the picture."

"Get a work sheet from the teacher."

e. Decorate the folder with desired pictures/drawings.

f. Laminate.

Hint: Use like-color folder and poster background for the picture in case the two become separated.

e. Laminate the picture and the folder.

f. Use an X-ACTO® knife to slit the folder pockets.

g. Design a work sheet to go with the picture and make a classroom set.

h. Store picture in left pocket, work sheets in right pocket.

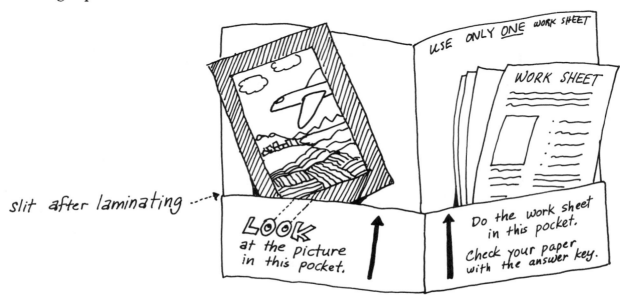

3. INDIVIDUALIZED PRACTICE FOLDERS – Students can practice rhyming words, contractions, abbreviations, compound words, math problems, vocabulary terms, etc., by matching game pieces to pieces glued inside a folder.

4. MAP-READING ACTIVITY FOLDERS – Cut small, colorful maps from old textbooks or workbooks. Glue each map on the left-inside of a file folder. Cut two naugahyde pockets. On the right side of the folder, plan side-by-side spots for the pockets. Under one area print, "True"; under the other area print, "False." Laminate the folder. Staple the two pockets in place. On strip tags write true/false questions for each map. Construct an answer key to make the folder self-checking. Laminate strip tags and answer key.

An alternative to the pockets is to use the work sheet idea in number 2, page 45.

5. POETRY FILE FOLDERS – Collect poems to accompany a certain unit or for creative writing time. Glue a poem to the left-inside of the folder. On the right side, provide instructions for a variety of activities to accompany the poem such as, "Write a poem of your own on this same subject," or "Put yourself in the place of one of the characters in the poem and write a paragraph to tell what you would do."

Laminate all poetry folders and gather them in a brightly covered box marked "POETRY BOX." Place on a shelf for extra-credit time or for use at a specific time.

Read each card. Put the card in the correct pocket. Check your answer with the answer key.

IS THERE A RAILROAD?

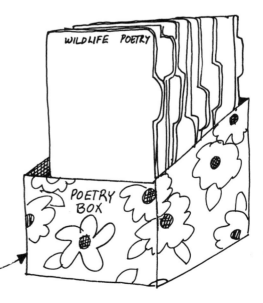

WILDLIFE POETRY

POETRY BOX

Detergent box covered in adhesive paper

Blue Folders

LIBERTY BELL

Statue of Liberty

Red Folders

Yellow Folders

America's Flag

COLOR-CODE BY CONTENT OR READING LEVEL

For example, in a unit on American symbols, use red folders for articles on the flag, blue folders for articles on the Liberty Bell, and yellow folders for articles on the Statue of Liberty, etc.

8. READING FILE FOLDERS – These will help meet the reading needs of all students in the classroom. If you have a sixth-grade student who reads on third-grade level, you cannot give that student a third-grade book. The humiliation would be too much! But you can cut articles from children's magazines. Laminate the pages of the articles separately. Decorate the front of a file folder and laminate it. Then staple the article into the folder.

If you collect a number of articles that will go with one unit of study, make an extra-credit "READING BOX" to go with the unit. Create a work sheet that can be used with any article in the box.

6. BOOK REPORT FILE FOLDERS – Check with the school librarian to see if book jackets are available. Trim and glue book jackets to front of file folders. On inside-left of the folder, glue the book flap that summarizes the book. If flap is unavailable, print a brief summary of your own. On right side of the folder, list activities to be carried out in a book report.

7. COLOR-CODING WITH FILE FOLDERS – Distinguish among reading file folders at various reading levels by using one color for upper-level articles, another color for grade-level articles, and a third color for low-level articles.

Materials for a unit that has distinct parts can be color-coded for easy sorting.

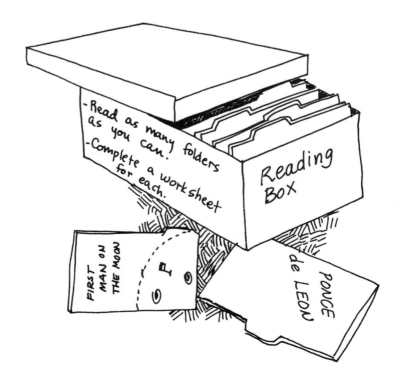

- Read as many folders as you can.
- Complete a worksheet for each.

Reading Box

FIRST MAN ON THE MOON

PONCE de LEON

Reading Box Work Sheet

1. Title of the article you read.

   _____

2. Do you think this was a good title? Why or why not?

   _____

3. Write another title that you think would fit this article.

   _____

4. If the article has a main character, what is his/her name? Describe the main character.

   _____

5. Where does the article take place? _____

6. Write the main idea of the article.

   _____

7. Why do you think the author wrote this article?

   _____
   _____

8. Which part of the article did you like best? Why?

   _____
   _____

9. Which part of the article did you like least? Why?

   _____
   _____

10. Write a different ending for the article.

    _____

11. If you were writing this article, what part would you leave out? Why?

    _____

12. If you were writing this article, what would you add that the writer has left out? Why?

    _____

13. Why do you think this article is included in the reading box for this unit?

    _____

14. Find and list ten additional facts about this subject which are not included in this article.

    _____
    _____
    _____

NOTE: These questions can be adjusted according to the students' ages.

Now That I've Made It— Where Can I Keep It?

Are you that lucky teacher who has all the storage space you need? Of course not! It is doubtful there is such a teacher. Even one who starts out with adequate storage soon finds that all space has been filled and more is needed.

Teachers seem to be born pack rats. This condition leads to an unending accumulation of "stuff" which leads to "move-and-shuffle," a sort of ritual that teachers constantly perform to try to make room for everything they use or "might use some day."

As teachers get hooked on creating, there are more things all the time that have to be stored somewhere.

HELPS FOR THE STORAGE PROBLEM

1. A large, flat area is needed to store game boards. If you don't have a big shelf, contact companies that deal in paper products. Boxes that poster board come in are about 25" x 30" x 4" and are quite sturdy – ideal for storing game boards. Keep the box on the floor of a closet or under a table.

2. Game boards are more easily stored if they are constructed in two halves as illustrated.

3. For storing game pieces, cards, and answer keys, use the small, sturdy boxes suggested in the materials list on page 9. (Be sure the box will hold the answer key and a spinner if there is one.) Cover boxes with bright self-adhesive paper and label each box with the name of the game. A bookshelf will look nice stacked with all the brightly covered boxes, and they will be accessible to students.

4. A unique container for storing game pieces is an empty unmarked margarine tub. Use the lid to construct the spinner; store game markers and cards inside the tub.

GAMES, IDEAS, AND INSPIRATIONS

PICK-A-POCKET

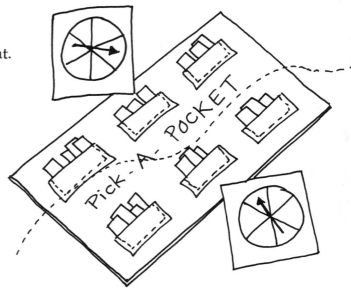

GRADE LEVEL
Use with any grade level by varying content.

PURPOSE
To review any unit content.

MATERIALS NEEDED:
- 1 poster board (22" x 28")
- 2 heavy poster board squares (9" x 9")
- 1 poster board strip (1" x 4")
- 6 naugahyde pockets (4" x 5")
- 2 flathead stove bolts
- unlined index cards (5" x 8")
- compass
- box to hold strip tags and spinners
- self-adhesive paper to cover box

CONSTRUCTION

1. Across the center of the large poster, letter the title, "Pick-A-Pocket."

2. Arrange pockets in position. (Do not staple yet.)

3. Under each pocket, number from one to six.

4. Make two spinners according to directions on page 35. Number spinner segments one to six in random order.

5. Determine six categories to be reviewed. (See suggested list on page 53.) Write review questions to fit all categories.

6. Mark each index card into sections 1" x 5". On each segment, write one review question. Number each question.

7. Make an answer key. Use one index card per category. Be sure to print name of category at top of card.

8. Laminate index cards on which questions are printed. Cut the cards into strip tags.

9. Laminate board and answer keys.

10. Staple naugahyde pockets to board.

11. Cover storage box with self-adhesive paper.

PLAYERS
Two teams with any number of students.
One scorekeeper.

PROCEDURE
1. Hang game board on bulletin board. On chalkboard, write a key to the categories for the game.

2. Each team spins to determine the number of the pocket from which a question must be answered. (Pass spinner to each team member in turn.)

3. Teacher or game leader reads the question. (If the teacher does not lead the game, the scorekeeper would also serve as judge, reading correct answers from the key.)

4. A correct answer gains a point for the team, and play moves to opposing team.

5. If answer is incorrect, strip is returned to pocket for another turn.

6. The winning team is the one with the most points when all pockets are empty or at the end of a specified time limit.

VARIATION
Construct game with fewer pockets for younger children. Adjust numbers on spinners accordingly.

SUGGESTED CATEGORIES FOR STRIP TAGS

SCIENCE
Desert
Ocean
Jungle
Space
Mountains
Plains

SOCIAL STUDIES
People
Places
Things
Events
Vocabulary
Guess What?

MATH
Addition
Subtraction
Multiplication
Division
Estimations
Guess What?

UNITED STATES
Spell the state
Locate on map
Capitals
State abbreviations
Geographic features
Products

ENGLISH
Synonyms
Antonyms
Syllables
Plurals
Contractions
Abbreviations

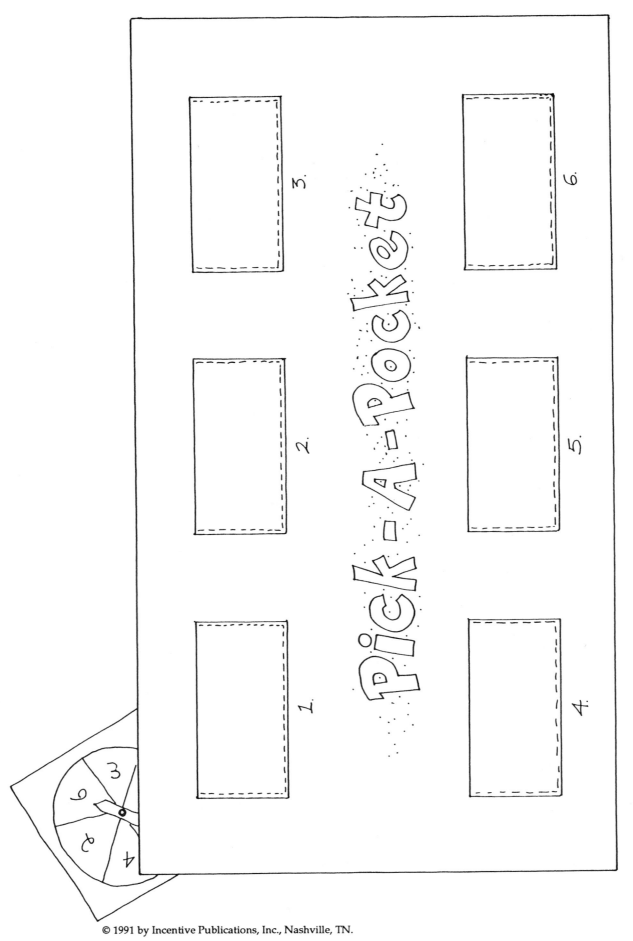

Pick-A-Pocket

IN A SPIN!

GRADE LEVEL
3-6

PURPOSE
To review any skill or content.

MATERIALS NEEDED:
- 1 white poster board (18" x 20")
- 1 scrap of poster board (1" x 6")
- game board pattern
- 1 flathead stove bolt
- construction paper
- index cards (5" x 8")
- large envelope to hold lists and answer keys

CONSTRUCTION
1. Use opaque projector to enlarge and transfer illustrated game board to poster.

2. Cut one end of a 1" x 6" poster board to a point to make an arrow.

3. Laminate board and arrow.

4. Make a hole in the center of the spinner and the arrow.

5. Insert bolt through center of spinner from underside. Drop arrow on bolt. Affix nut.

6. Make lists of spelling words, vocabulary terms, questions, math problems, etc. Each list should have sixteen items. (Read "Variation I" on page 56.)

7. Mount each list on construction paper.

8. Make an answer key for each list.

9. Laminate lists and answer keys.

PLAYERS
Two players (or two teams)
One questioner, judge, and scorekeeper

PROCEDURE

1. Player (or team leader) spins.

2. Number landed on determines which item on the list the player must answer.

3. If player lands on a number already used, spin again (or follow procedure in "Variation II" below).

4. Judge reads the item from the list aloud.

5. A correct answer gains a point.

6. An incorrect answer subtracts a point and gives opponent a chance to answer in addition to taking his/her own turn.

7. When all items have been answered or at the end of a specified time, the player (or team) with the most points is declared the winner.

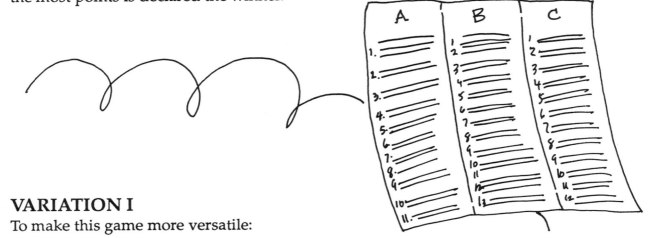

VARIATION I

To make this game more versatile:

For each number (1-16) on the list, make three questions lettered "a," "b," and "c." When player spins a "3," for example, he/she answers "3a." Another student landing on "3" could answer with "3b," etc.

VARIATION II

In each segment of the spinner, print two different numbers (see illustration on page 58) so that a list of thirty-two items can be used. When student lands on the segment numbered "2" and "32," for example, he/she may answer either question "2" or "32." However, if "2" has already been answered, he/she must answer "32." If both have been answered, player spins again.

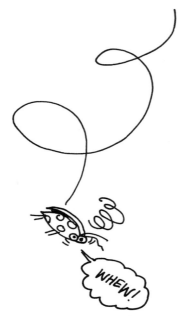

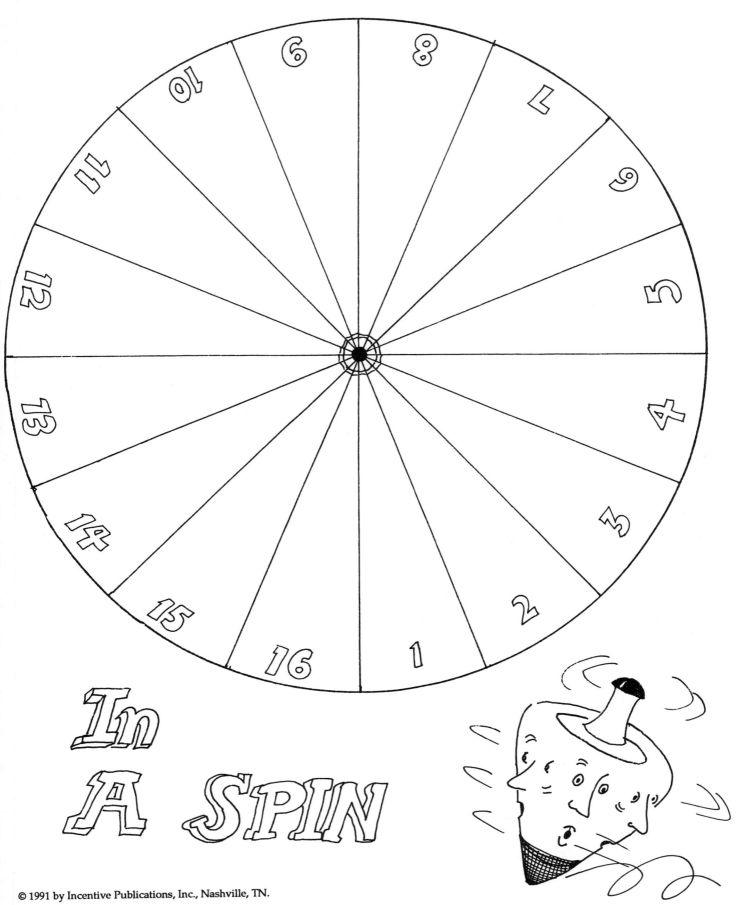

In A SPIN

In A Spin

GO!

GRADE LEVEL
1-3

PURPOSE
To practice directions, north, south, east, west. (This is a good outside activity.)

MATERIALS NEEDED:
- 1 poster board (18" x 20")
- 1 poster board scrap (1" x 6")
- game board pattern
- 1 flathead stove bolt
- pictures to decorate game board

CONSTRUCTION
1. Using opaque projector, transfer and enlarge illustrated game board to fill large poster.

2. Decorate as desired.

3. Make arrow from poster board scrap.

4. Laminate board and arrow. Make hole in center of arrow and spinner.

5. Insert bolt through center of spinner from underside. Drop arrow on bolt. Affix nut.

PLAYERS
Small group or whole class under teacher-direction.

PROCEDURE
1. Move chairs and other obstacles so students can walk in all directions. Children sit around the edge of the room.

2. One player comes to the center of the room, spins, reads the directions to which the arrow points, and takes that number of steps in the proper direction.

3. A move in the wrong direction means the player must return to his/her seat, and the next player takes a turn.

4. Play continues for a given period of time or until one player reaches a wall and is declared the winner.

Hint: If a large group is playing, keep track of whose turn it is by giving each player a number tag to wear. Turns are then taken in number sequence.

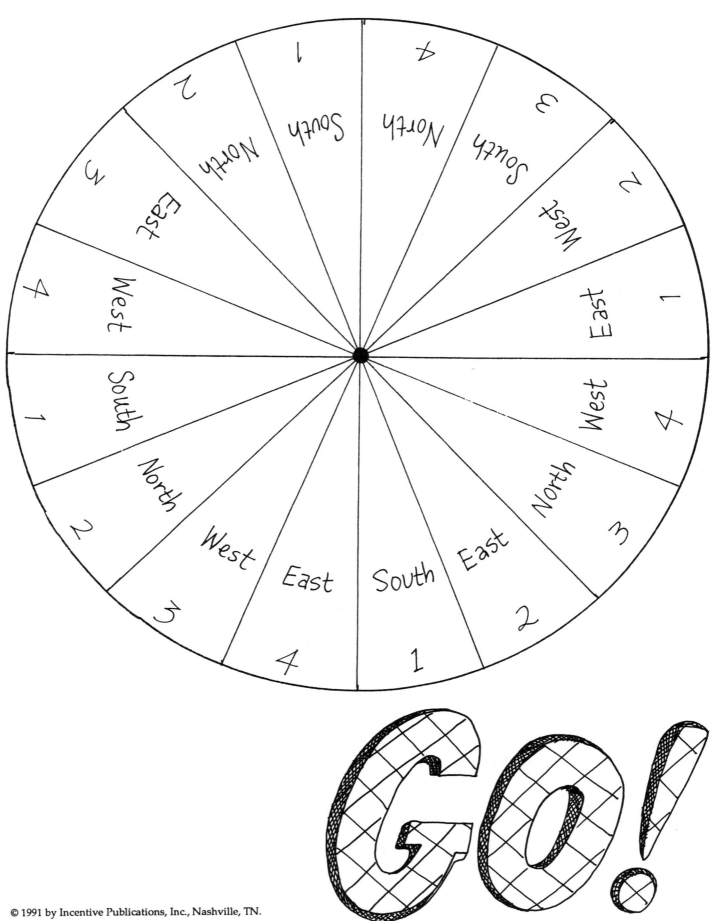

SCARECROW PATCHES

GRADE LEVEL
1-6 (depending on game cards used)

PURPOSE
To practice and review any skill or content. (Suggestions given are for rhyming words in primary grades.)

MATERIALS NEEDED:
- 1 white poster board (20" x 22")
- construction paper
- index card (5" x 8")
- scarecrow and patch patterns
- 4 game markers
- box to hold game pieces
- self-adhesive paper to cover box

CONSTRUCTION

1. With opaque projector, enlarge and transfer scarecrow pattern on page 64 to fill large poster board.

2. Color the scarecrow. (A tan face will suggest burlap.)

3. From construction paper, cut game cards ("patches"). These should be about 4" x 4", but a little irregularity in size will make the patches look more interesting. With black marker, "fray" the edges of each patch. (See illustration on page 62.)

4. Print vocabulary words, math problems, etc., on patches. Print the correct answer on the back of each card. In the lower right corner of the back, print instructions for forward movement, "Move 1," "Move 2," "Move 3." Use more 1's than 2's, and use 3's sparingly.

5. On one card, print the word "PATCHES." Use this as a cover card for the game stack.

NOTE: This cover card is important! Since words and problems are on the faces of the game cards, students will constantly look ahead to see what their own game problem will be. Use of the game cover "PATCH" will prevent this.

REMINDER: Save time spent in sorting game cards by color-coding: all math questions on red, rhyming words on blue, social studies vocabulary words on yellow, etc.

6. On some patches, print penalties and rewards in keeping with the scarecrow theme. (Those suggested on page 63 should be simplified for primary grades.)

7. Print rules on index card.

8. Laminate all game pieces.

9. Cover a storage box with self-adhesive paper.

PLAYERS
Two to four.

PROCEDURE
a. Stack "patches" faceup on front of scarecrow's shirt. Top with the PATCHES cover card.

b. Each player, in turn, takes a patch, replaces cover card, lays his/her card on table so the back cannot be seen, and reads the word or problem aloud.

c. After giving an answer, he/she turns the card over and reads the correct answer aloud.

d. If correct, the player moves forward as instructed on the card.

e. The first player to go around the scarecrow is the winner.

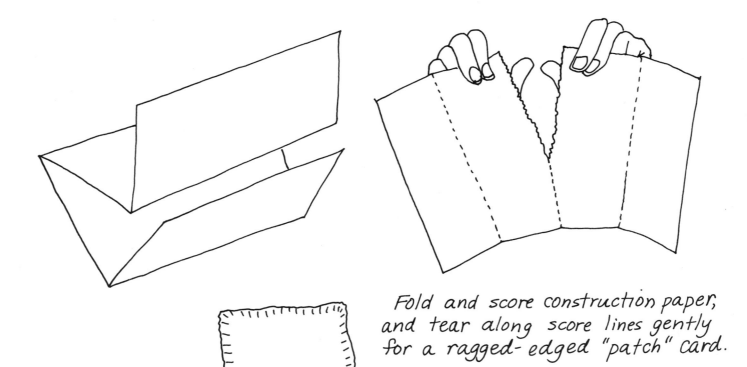

Fold and score construction paper, and tear along score lines gently for a ragged-edged "patch" card.

SUGGESTED RHYMING WORDS FOR SCARECROW PATCHES

1. back — track — black
2. cake — make — break
3. car — star — far
4. brick — stick — lick
5. hook — brook — took
6. blue — true — shoe
7. crumb — plum — drum
8. bring — sting — wing
9. ball — fall — wall
10. cat — bat — mat
11. dog — frog — log
12. dish — wish — fish
13. tie — fly — sigh
14. three — bee — see
15. test — best — nest
16. beef — leaf — chief
17. cart — heart — smart
18. blow — show — tow
19. coat — boat — wrote
20. glass — pass — grass
21. rose — toes — bows
22. queen — bean — green
23. price — rice — slice
24. school — pool — tool
25. star — car — far

...rose.... toes... bows...

SUGGESTIONS FOR PENALTY AND REWARD CARDS

1. You went to sleep in the haystack. Lose one turn.
2. You took the scarecrow's hat as a joke. Go back three spaces.
3. You think the scarecrow is ugly. Go back two spaces.
4. You helped Farmer Brown mend the scarecrow. Take an extra turn.
5. You took a friend to see the scarecrow. Go ahead two spaces.

You went to sleep in the haystack.

LOSE ONE TURN.

64

RAIN, RAIN, GO AWAY

GRADE LEVEL
1-3

PURPOSE
To practice forming plurals.

MATERIALS NEEDED:
- 2 white poster boards (each 11" x 14")
- light blue construction paper
- patterns – frog, umbrella, raindrop
- 1 index card (5" x 8")

CONSTRUCTION
1. Color umbrella and frog patterns as desired. Cut out.

2. Glue patterns to white poster boards.

3. Using the raindrop pattern, outline fifteen raindrops above each umbrella.

4. Cut thirty raindrops, same size as pattern, from light blue construction paper.

5. Print a word to be made plural on each raindrop. Include a variety of words that must add "s," "es," and "ies." Number each word.

6. Use index card to make answer key.

7. Laminate all pieces.

PLAYERS
Two players and one judge.

PROCEDURE
1. Each player has his/her own board.

2. Place fifteen blue raindrops facedown on each board covering the outlines drawn above the umbrellas.

3. Each player, in turn, lifts a raindrop from his/her board, tells the number of the word, then gives the plural of the word.

4. The judge checks the answer.

5. If correct, the player keeps that raindrop, and his/her opponent takes his/her turn.

6. If an incorrect answer is given, that raindrop is replaced on the board to be attempted at a later turn. (The player must not pick up this same raindrop on the very next turn but must do some others first.)

7. The first player to make it "stop raining" by removing all the raindrops from his/her board is declared the winner.

VARIATION

Raindrops are placed word-side down on the table.

Each player, in turn, reads the word, tells the plural, and (if correct), places the raindrop on his/her opponent's board.

The first player to make it "start raining" on his/her opponent wins the game.

VOCABULARY FLIP

GRADE LEVEL
1-6 (depending on words used)

PURPOSE
To review vocabulary.

MATERIALS NEEDED:
- 1 cardboard piece (10" x 18")
- self-adhesive paper
- construction paper
- 2 metal rings (1.5" in diameter)
- clear packaging tape

CONSTRUCTION
1. Cover both sides of cardboard piece with self-adhesive paper.

2. Following the step-by-step illustration, fold the cardboard, secure with tape.

3. Punch holes with an ice pick or a pencil. Enlarge holes by working pick/pencil in circular motion.

4. Using cards in horizontal position, print one vocabulary word on each card centered.

5. On the back of each vocabulary card, print the word's definition UPSIDE DOWN and centered.

6. Laminate cards.

7. Above the vocabulary word on each card, punch two holes to correspond with the holes punched in the triangular stand.

8. Using metal rings, hang vocabulary cards with words facing out on the triangle board.

PLAYERS
One – for individual practice.
Three or four – for small group practice.

PROCEDURE

1. Each player needs pencil and paper to write definitions. One student should keep score for the group.

2. Each student writes the definition for the word displayed.

3. One student lifts the card for all to see the correct definition.

4. The scorekeeper records a point for each student having the correct definition.

5. Optional: For an incorrect definition, a point is subtracted from the score. (At times a student might have a negative score.)

6. Follow the same procedure until all words are used or until allotted time is gone. The student who has the most points is the winner.

Make several vocabulary Flip-Its. Divide the class into several groups, provide each group with a Flip-It, and have a vocabulary review hour for the entire class.

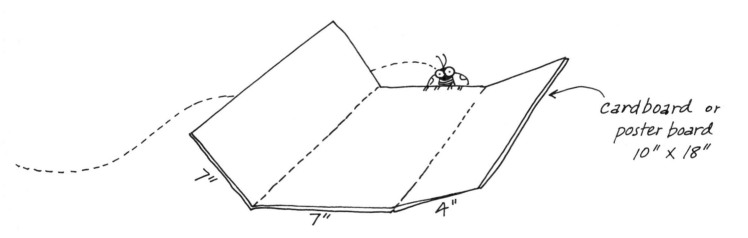

cardboard or poster board 10" x 18"

7"

7"

4"

Cover cardboard with self-adhesive paper.
Fold on scored marks.
Secure open edge with strip of clear packaging tape.

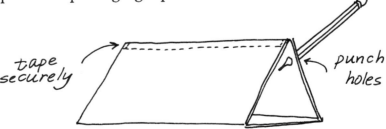

tape securely

punch holes

Hang vocabulary word cards on the Flip-It as illustrated on page 70.

69

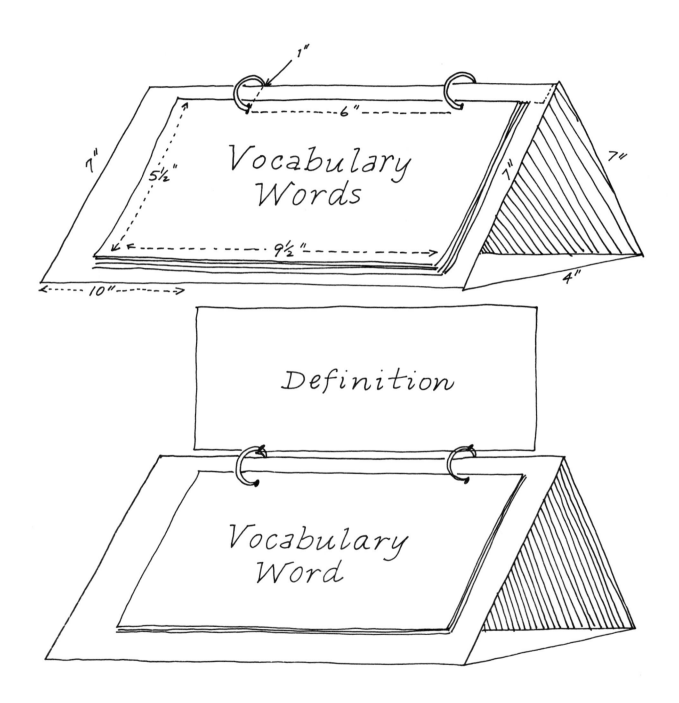

Vocabulary Words

Definition

Vocabulary Word

COMMUNITY HELPERS FLIP-IT

GRADE LEVEL
K-2

PURPOSE
To reinforce knowledge of community
helpers by matching pictures and vocabulary.

MATERIALS NEEDED:
- 1 piece cardboard (20" x 30")
- self-adhesive paper
- 30 index cards (4" x 6")
- 6 metal snap-open rings 1.5" in diameter
- pictures from old workbooks

NOTE: Find ten pictures of people dressed
to fit specific careers and ten pictures of tools or
implements used in those same careers.

SUGGESTED PICTURE COMBINATIONS

Policeman: Whistle
Mailman: Letter
Dentist: Hand Mirror/Chair
Secretary: Typewriter
Fireman: Hat/Boots
Waitress: Menu
Doctor: Stethescope
Janitor: Push broom
Nurse: Thermometer/Injection Syringe
Teacher: Chalkboard

CONSTRUCTION

1. Using 4" x 6" cards vertically, glue pictures to twenty cards.

2. On the ten remaining cards, print names of ten careers to fit the pictures used.

3. For self-checking, mark matching sets of cards on the back with a symbol. (For example, the picture of the nurse, the word "nurse," and the picture of the thermometer could all be marked with a plus symbol (+). The picture of the fireman, the word "fireman," and the picture of the fireman's hat could all be marked with an "O."

4. Laminate the cards.

5. Punch two holes in the top of each card 3 1/2" apart.

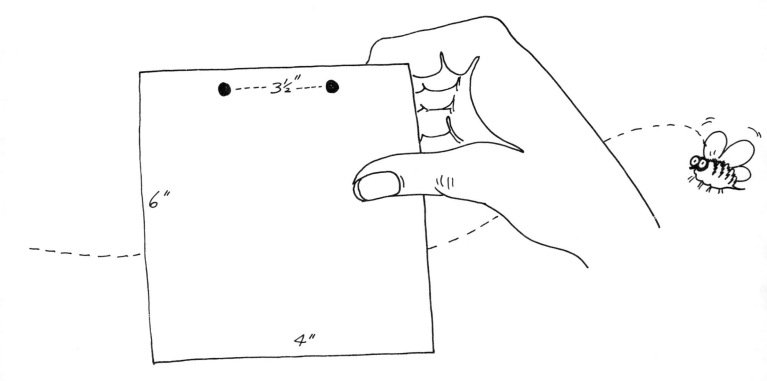

Hint: Do not punch until after laminating to prevent punching twice.

6. Make Flip-It according to illustration on pages 68-70.

7. Shuffle card stacks. Use metal rings to fasten the card stacks to the Flip-It.

PLAYERS
One – for individual practice.
Small group or entire class under teacher-direction.

PROCEDURE
Student matches pictures. In group or class situation, follow matching with discussion.

VARIATION
A change of cards makes this activity suitable for a wide range of matching activities and age groups.

Make several Flip-Its for students to use in spare time.

Make Flip-Its to match pairs as well as triplets.

SUGGESTED TOPICS FOR FLIP-ITS

1. State outline, name of state, state capital.

2. Colors and color words.

3. Numerals, number words, dots. (3, three, ...)

4. Things that go together. (3 animals, 3 foods, 3 trees, 3 tools, mom/dad/baby)

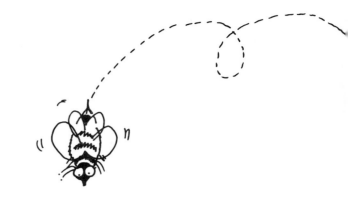

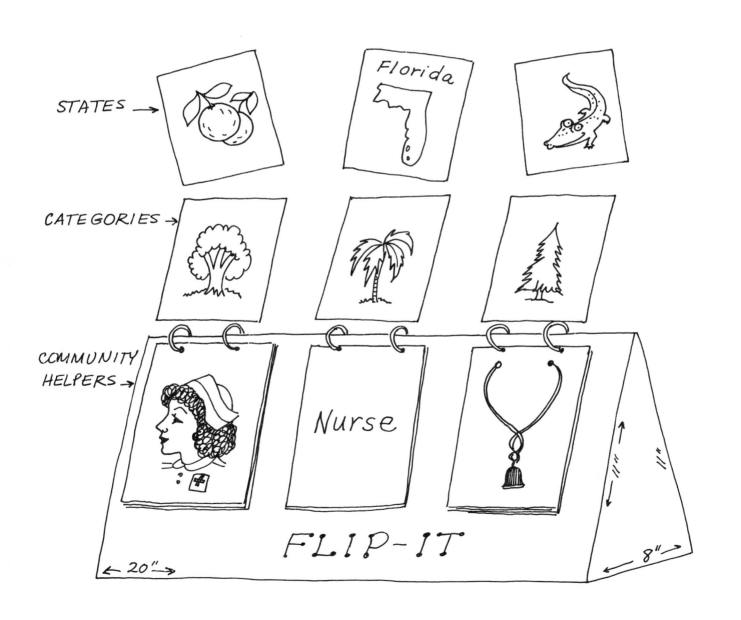

HANG-A-WORD

GRADE LEVEL
1-6 (depending on vocabulary used)

PURPOSE
To review vocabulary.

MATERIALS NEEDED:
- 1 white poster board (20" x 22")
- index cards (5" x 8")
- 1 piece naugahyde (4" x 5")
- brads
- pictures (optional)

CONSTRUCTION
1. Mark poster board into sections and segments as illustrated.

2. In upper left corner, letter game title, "Hang-A-Word."

3. Print words to be defined and instructions on the board as shown in the illustration.

4. Decorate board with attention-getting pictures, if desired.

5. Mark 5" x 8" index cards into segments (each 1" x 5"), and print one definition in each segment. IMPORTANT: LEAVE A 1" MARGIN AT LEFT EDGE OF EACH DEFINITION SEGMENT.

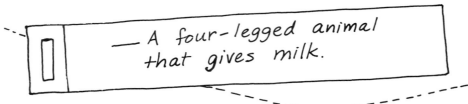

6. Laminate game board and 5" x 8" cards on which definitions are printed.

7. Use an X-ACTO® knife to cut a 1/4" x 1/2" rectangle in the 1" margin at the left edge of each definition strip.

8. Cut definition strips apart.

9. Use an X-ACTO® knife to make small horizontal slits in the game board as shown in the illustration.

10. Affix a brad to the game board in each of these slits.

11. Staple the naugahyde pocket to the game board.

12. Make an answer key on an index card. Laminate.

PLAYERS
One – for individual practice
Two students may work together
Small group – under teacher-direction

PROCEDURE
1. Hang poster on a bulletin board at eye level.

2. Place definition strips in naugahyde pocket.

3. Place one or two student chairs facing the bulletin board.

4. Students will perform as indicated in the written instructions and at times specified by the teacher. (For example, "Students, each of you is expected to do this vocabulary board some time during the next two weeks.")

DIRECTIONS
1. Take definition strips from the pocket.

2. Hang the definition by the correct word.

3. Check your work with answer key.

4. Copy all words and definitions on paper.

5. Turn in your paper.

6. You may use the dictionary if you need help.

NOTE: Step 6 is optional.

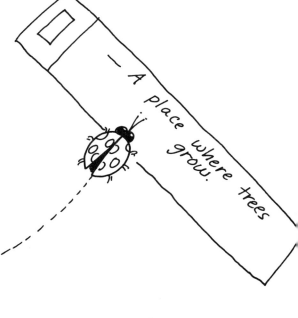

VARIATIONS
For very young children, cut colored strips and put color words on the board, or put numbers on the board and number words on the strips. Practice rhyming words, contractions, or other word skills.

Instead of calling this game "Hang-A-Word," name it according to the content of the vocabulary. Use suggestions as follows:

MAP WORDS – Cut the title words from maps in an old atlas. Define words and terms connected with maps.

MONEY – Make title words out of pictures of coins cut from old workbooks. On definition tags, glue a picture of a coin. On the board, print names of money.

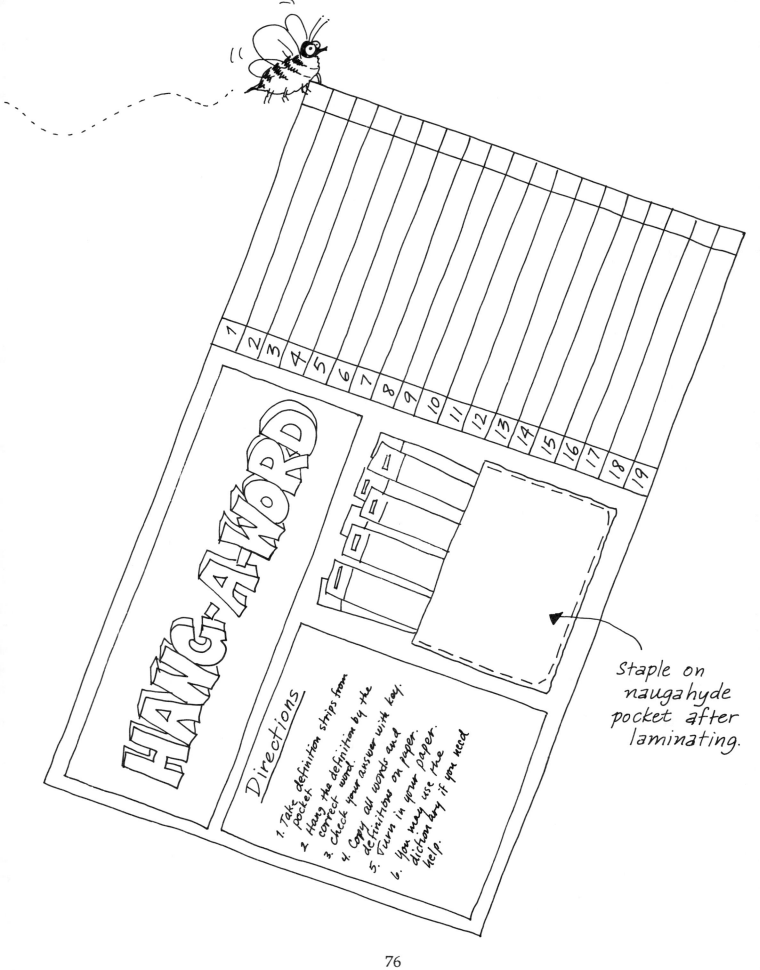

HANG-A-WORD

Directions

1. Take definition strips from pocket.
2. Hang the definition by the correct word.
3. Check your answer with key.
4. Copy all words and definitions on paper.
5. Turn in your paper.
6. You may use the dictionary if you need help.

Staple on naugahyde pocket after laminating.

1 2 3 4 5 6 7 8 9 10 11 12 13 14 15 16 17 18 19

TOSS A SYL-LA-"BALL"

GRADE LEVEL
3-6

PURPOSE
To practice recognition of syllables.

MATERIALS NEEDED:
- 1 white poster board (18" x 22")
- patterns – seal and ball
- construction paper – yellow and pink
- 4 pieces naugahyde (3" x 5")
- 2 index cards (5" x 8")

CONSTRUCTION

1. Make four copies of the seal pattern. Color, accenting each seal with a different color. Number seal stands one through four. Cut out.

2. As illustrated, glue seals along the poster board evenly spaced. Leave room for a pocket under each seal and for a game title along the top.

3. Letter game title on the board.

4. Using the ball pattern, cut twenty-five yellow and twenty-five pink circles from construction paper.

5. On yellow circles, print words of one, two, three, and four syllables. Repeat on pink circles in same ratio, that is, have the same number of one syllable words, two syllable words, etc., on both pink and yellow circles.

6. If there will be an answer key, shuffle all word cards together and then number from one through fifty. (Shuffle well in order to avoid having many words of the same number of syllables listed together on the answer key.)

7. Make the answer key on an index card.

8. Print the rules on an index card.

9. Laminate all pieces.

10. Staple the four naugahyde pieces under the seals to make four pockets.

PLAYERS

One – individual practice
Two players and one judge
Small group – under teacher-direction

PROCEDURE

(For two players)

1. Affix game to bulletin board at eye level (or use flat on a tabletop).

2. One student uses pink circles and the other uses yellow circles.

3. Each student shuffles his/her cards and stacks them facedown.

4. In turn, each student picks up the top card from his/her stack, reads the number on the card (for the judge), reads the words aloud, and tells how many syllables the word has.

5. The judge gives the correct answer.

6. If correct, player puts the circle in the pocket under the appropriate seal.

7. Circles identified incorrectly are placed in a discard pile.

8. Winner is determined by the number of circles of his/her color that are in the pockets.

VARIATIONS

Shuffle all cards together in one stack. Players alternate turns and keep score on paper gaining one point for each correct answer and losing one point for each incorrect answer.

For younger grades, construct the game with only two or three seals.

TOSS-A-SYL-LA-"BALL"

Design a game board using this illustration as a model.

THE STRAWBERRY PATCH

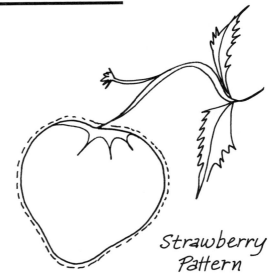

Strawberry Pattern

GRADE LEVEL
3-6

PURPOSE
To practice synonyms.

MATERIALS NEEDED:
- 1 white poster board (18" x 22")
- white index cards, unlined (5" x 8")
- 2 small white margarine tubs (optional)
- 2 pieces red yarn about 9" long (optional)
- patterns – strawberry, game board

CONSTRUCTION

1. Using an opaque projector, transfer the strawberry patch game board to the large white poster board.

2. With a green marker, color the vine and the leaves.

3. Outline each strawberry with a red marker and put on seed dots. Do NOT color strawberries.

4. Using the strawberry pattern, draw and cut out twenty-nine strawberries from the white index cards.

5. Color both sides of each strawberry – red for the berry and green for the leafy top.

6. On each strawberry print a word. Number each one for checking purposes.

7. On an index card, make an answer key printing synonyms for the words on the berries.

8. Laminate board, berries, and answer key.

9. OPTIONAL — To make a strawberry basket for each player to collect the berries picked, punch a hole in either side of each small margarine tub. Tie a red yarn handle on each basket.

PLAYERS
Two players and one judge.

PROCEDURE

1. All berries are placed word-side down on the board.

2. In turn, each player picks up a strawberry from any spot on the board, reads aloud the number of the card (for the judge), and then reads the word. He/she then gives a synonym for the word.

3. The judge reads the correct answer.

4. If correct, the player places the strawberry in his/her basket.

5. If incorrect, the opposing player has a chance to give a synonym for this same berry, collect the berry, and then take his/her own turn following the same procedure.

6. Play continues until all the berries have been "picked."

7. The winner is the player with the most berries in his/her basket.

VARIATIONS

1. Read the word; give an antonym.

2. Read the vocabulary word; give the definition.

3. Read the word; divide into syllables.

4. If the word is misspelled, spell it correctly.

5. Read the word; give the plural.

6. Read the word; give a homonym.

7. Read the math problem; solve it.

For individual practice: lay out all the strawberries with words faceup, and place them on the board in alphabetical order following the vine.

Use the board like a remembering game. Place fourteen pairs of words facedown. Player turns up two berries at a time attempting to make a match. A correct match allows the player to put the two matching berries in his/her basket and try for another match.

Use the strawberries as a game trail starting at upper left and going to the end of the vine. Use any question cards desired.

SUGGESTED SYNONYMS FOR STRAWBERRIES

1. happy – glad
2. dad – father, daddy
3. pretty – beautiful
4. sack – bag
5. easy – simple
6. car – automobile
7. small – little, tiny
8. street – road
9. finish – end
10. cry – weep
11. naughty – bad

12. mend – fix, repair
13. listen – hear
14. noisy – loud
15. huge – big, large
16. thin – slender, slim
17. begin – start
18. quit – stop
19. grandmother – granny
20. mom – mother, momma, ma
21. couch – sofa

22. mistake – error
23. leap – jump
24. ill – sick
25. kids – children
26. smart – bright
27. house – home
28. frighten – scare
29. grin – smile
30. leave – go
31. arrive – come
32. hurt – ache

The Strawberry Patch

83

BRING ME FLOWERS

GRADE LEVEL
2-4

PURPOSE
To practice classifying types of sentences.

MATERIALS NEEDED:
- 3 white poster boards (10" x 14")
- patterns – 2 boys, 1 girl, flower
- 3 naugahyde pockets (3" x 5")
- 4 metal rings (1" diameter) or yarn
- construction paper (pastel colors)
- 2 index cards (5" x 8")
- box to hold game pieces
- self-adhesive paper to cover box

CONSTRUCTION

1. Color boy and girl patterns. Cut out.

2. Glue boy and girl patterns to poster board (1 figure per board) leaving room under figure for pocket.

3. Print lettering and punctuation on each board as illustrated.

4. Laminate posters.

5. Staple a naugahyde pocket to each board.

6. Arrange posters as illustrated, punch matching holes, and put together with rings or yarn.

7. Cut twenty-four flowers, all one color or a variety of spring colors.

8. On the flowers, print statements of love, caring, and sharing – eight declarative statements, eight questions, eight exclamatory statements. (See suggested list of statements on page 85.) Number each flower. (IMPORTANT: Be sure to omit punctuation on flower statements.)

9. Laminate and cut out flowers.

10. On index cards, print rules and answer key. Laminate.

11. With self-adhesive paper, cover storage box.

PLAYERS
Two players
One judge
Or use with small group under teacher-direction

PROCEDURE
1. Stand board on table in front of players. Place flower cards upside down.

2. In turn, each player takes a flower, reads the statement aloud, and tells what kind of sentence it is.

3. Judge reads correct answer from key.

4. If correct, player puts the flower in the appropriate pocket.

5. Judge records one point for the player.

6. Second player takes a turn following same procedure.

7. A player who gives an incorrect answer buries that flower in the pile, and play moves to the opponent.

8. When all flowers have been used, the player having the most points is the winner.

VARIATION
Make flowers of two colors, one stack for each player. Flowers identified correctly are placed in appropriate pocket. Winner is determined by the number of flowers each player has in the pockets. This eliminates the need for keeping score.

SUGGESTED ITEMS FOR FLOWERS

DECLARATIVE STATEMENTS:
1. I have a gift for you
2. I have picked some pretty flowers
3. Valentine's Day is a time to be nice
4. We are going to a party
5. We should always be kind
6. I think flowers are pretty
7. I have many friends
8. I see big red flowers in the yard

QUESTIONS:
1. Will you give me a smile
2. Where are you going
3. What time is the party
4. Can you go with me
5. Will you be my Valentine
6. Do you like the flowers
7. Isn't the red flower pretty
8. Where did you get the flowers

EXCLAMATIONS:
1. Oh, I will be your Valentine
2. What fun this is
3. Oh, I do like the flowers
4. How nice you are
5. What a pretty dress
6. What a nice surprise
7. Oh, the flowers smell so good
8. Look, what big flowers

NOTE: Be sure that you do not put punctuation marks on the flower cards!

88

WORD FOLDERS

On the next few pages are ideas for constructing small word folders that can provide practice for a variety of word skills.

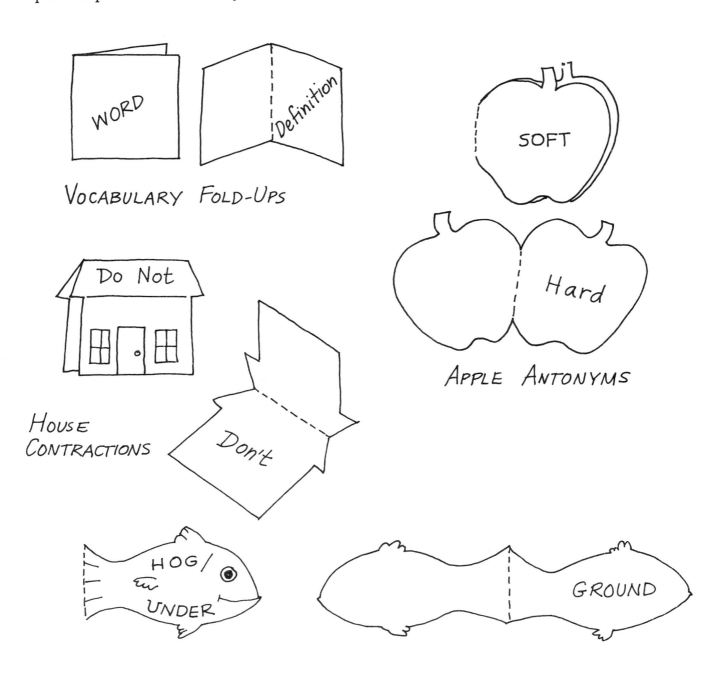

VOCABULARY FOLD-UPS

APPLE ANTONYMS

HOUSE CONTRACTIONS

HOUSE CONTRACTIONS

GRADE LEVEL
1-4

PURPOSE
To review and practice contractions.

MATERIALS NEEDED:
- construction paper
  (varied colors or just one color)
- house pattern
- index card (5" x 8")
- box to store finished houses
- self-adhesive paper to cover storage box

CONSTRUCTION
1. On construction paper, draw thirty houses the same size as the pattern (page 91).

2. Cut out each house and fold on the dotted line.

3. On the outside front of each house, draw door, windows, and roof line.

4. On the roof, print the two words to be contracted, for example, "WAS NOT."

5. On the inside, print the contraction, "WASN'T ."

6. Print rules on the 5" x 8" card.

7. Laminate all pieces. Fold and weight houses to press creases.

8. Cover storage box with self-adhesive paper.

PLAYERS
Two

PROCEDURE
1. Two players sit facing each other.

2. Each player holds half the house cards.

3. Player A holds up one closed card so that Player B can see only the two words on the front that he/she is to contract.

4. Player B reads the words aloud and then gives the contraction.

5. Player A opens the house to check and shows the correct answer to Player B.

6. If Player B gives the correct answer, he/she receives the house card and lays it aside to count for himself/herself.

7. This same procedure repeats in reverse with Player B showing a card to Player A.

8. Any cards not correctly answered are placed in a discard pile. These words may be reused when all other word folders have been claimed.

9. When all cards have been used, the player holding the largest number of houses is the winner.

CONTRACTIONS FOR USE ON HOUSES

Cannot, Can't
Is not, Isn't
Should not, Shouldn't
Were not, Weren't
Are not, Aren't
Could not, Couldn't
Has not, Hasn't
I am, I'm
She is, She's
He is, He's
It is, It's
We are, We're
You are, You're
They are, They're
I have, I've
You have, You've
We have, We've
They have, They've
I will, I'll
She will, She'll
He will, He'll
We will, We'll
You will, You'll
They will, They'll
Did not, Didn't
Would not, Wouldn't
Do not, Don't
Will not, Won't
Does not, Doesn't
Had not, Hadn't
Have not, Haven't

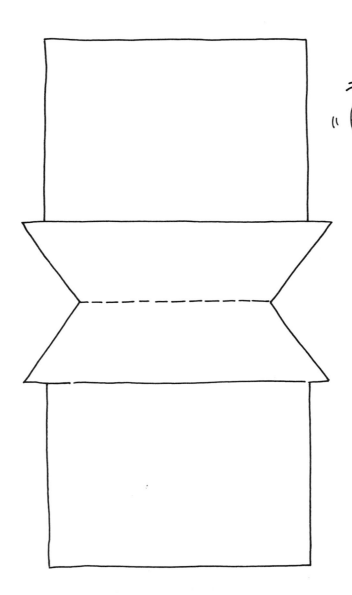

CAR ABBREVIATIONS

From colored folders or heavy construction paper, cut about fifty cars using the pattern given. Print selected word on the front of each car with abbreviation on the inside. Laminate and fold on the dotted line. Use as instructed for "House Contractions" on pages 90-91.

SUGGESTED ABBREVIATIONS FOR GRADES 4, 5, and 6

Mister – Mr	Senior – Sr.
Missus – Mrs.	Number – No.
Miss – Ms.	Inch – In.
Street – St.	Yard – Yd.
Boulevard – Blvd.	Foot – Ft.
Avenue – Ave.	Mile – Mi.
Route – Rt.	Page – Pg.
Road – Rd.	President – Pres.
Et Cetera – Etc.	Doctor – Dr.
Minute – Min.	Secretary – Sec.
Hour – Hr.	Principal – Prin.
Second – Sec.	School – Sch.
Railroad – RR	United States – U.S.
Junior – Jr.	America – Amer.

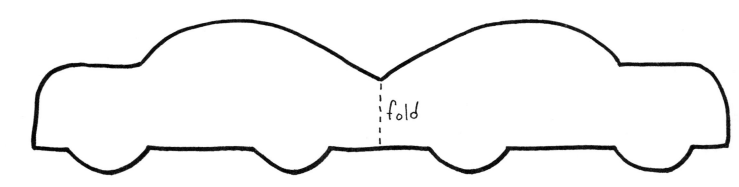

In addition to these, use abbreviations for the days of the week, the months of the year, your own city, nearby cities, and your home state. The largest cities in the United States could also be included.

fold

APPLE ANTONYMS

From red folders or heavy construction paper, cut thirty apples according to the pattern. Print selected word on the front of each apple with antonym on the inside. Laminate and fold on dotted line. Use according to directions given for "House Contractions" on pages 90-91. Use a list of words suitable to desired grade level.

SUGGESTED ANTONYMS

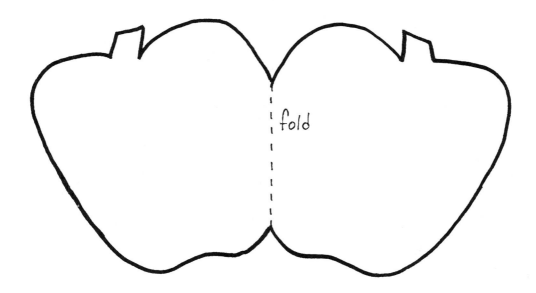

Short, Tall
Over, Under
Stop, Go
True, False
Plus, Minus
Dry, Wet
Good, Bad
Before, After
Hot, Cold
Hard, Soft
Empty, Full
Man, Woman
First, Last
Top, Bottom
High, Low

Come, Go
Right, Left
Black, White
Add, Subtract
Always, Never
Ask, Answer
Dark, Light
Big, Little
Open, Close
Push, Pull
Near, Far
Boy, Girl
Happy, Sad
Find, Lose
Front, Back

fold

FISH COMPOUNDS

From folders or heavy construction paper, cut thirty-two fish according to the pattern. Fold on dotted line. On the outside of each fish, print TWO WORDS that can be combined with ONE WORD printed on the inside of the fish. The inside word may fit at the beginning or the end of the word on the front.

EXAMPLE: HOG and UNDER on outside of fish will combine with GROUND on inside of fish to make GROUNDHOG and UNDERGROUND.

Laminate fish. Fold and weight under a heavy book. Use according to instructions for "House Contractions" on pages 90-91.

THIS IS NOT EASY and will provide a real challenge for better students at fifth and sixth grade levels.

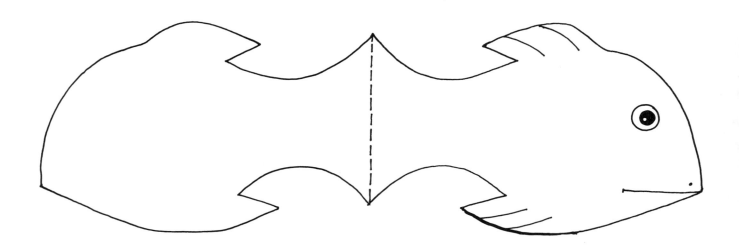

SUGGESTED WORD COMBINATIONS FOR FISH COMPOUNDS

OUTSIDE OF FOLDER   INSIDE OF FOLDER

case/worm	book
shore/shell	sea
corn/snow	flakes
snow/string	shoe
broom/yard	stick
head/house	light
law/jaw	breaker
base/foot	ball
soft/basket	ball
life/sail	boat
fire/out	side
cut/cake	short
steam/hard	ship
worm/quake	earth
mate/ground	play
hog/under	ground
moon/sun	light
work/school	house
bed/class	room
living/dining	room
my/your	self
head/tooth	ache
man/storm	snow
one/body	some/any
man/fly	fire
boat/fly	house
horse/butter	fly
sand/news	paper
muff/ring	ear
pot/cup	tea
ache/brush	tooth
cup/pan	cake

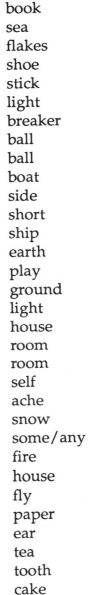

VARIATION ON SHAPED WORD FOLDERS

This activity can be constructed more simply by cutting square word folders rather than using patterns. Use a paper cutter to cut construction paper strips 6 inches long and 3 inches wide. Fold so that you have a 3 inch square.

ADDITIONAL SUGGESTIONS FOR WORD-FOLDER ACTIVITIES

Use word folders for any word skill such as:

VOCABULARY: Word on the outside; definition on the inside – or definition on the outside and word on the inside.

SPELLING: Is the word on the outside spelled correctly? Print "YES" or "NO" on the inside. If the answer is "NO," be sure to use the correct spelling.

UNIT REVIEW: Question on the outside; answer on the inside.

MATH: Problem on the outside; answers on the inside.

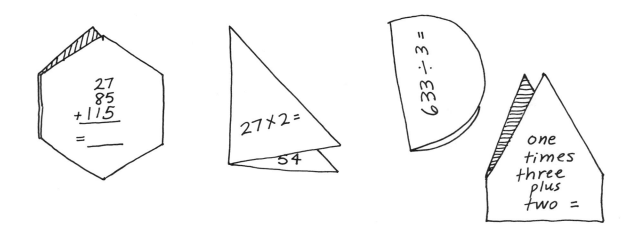

HEART-TO-HEART

GRADE LEVEL
K-4

PURPOSE
To practice categorizing fruits and vegetables.

MATERIALS NEEDED:
- 1 white poster board (16" x 18")
- red cutout hearts (or colorful Valentines)
- 2 pieces naugahyde (4" x 6")
- pink or red construction paper
- 2 index cards (5" x 8")

CONSTRUCTION

1. Cut two large red hearts from construction paper and glue them to the upper half of the large poster as illustrated.

2. Draw arrow.

3. Letter game title. (Be sure to leave room for pockets.) Along the bottom of the board (under the places where the pockets will be), letter "FRUITS" and "VEGETABLES."

4. Draw thirty hearts on the pink construction paper. (Do not cut hearts out until after laminating.)

5. On fifteen hearts, print items of one category, e.g., fruits. On fifteen hearts, print items of another category, e.g., vegetables. Number each heart.

6. Laminate board and sheets of hearts.

7. Cut out hearts.

8. Staple naugahyde pieces to bottom of game board.

9. On index cards, print rules and answer key.

PLAYERS

Two players and a judge.

PROCEDURE

1. Affix the game board to a bulletin board at eye level (or use flat on a tabletop).

2. Heart cards are stacked upside down in front of the players.

3. First player takes top heart, reads aloud the number of the card, and then the word. He/she then tells whether the named item is a fruit or vegetable.

4. The judge gives the correct answer.

5. If the player is correct, the judge records a point for the player who places the heart in the appropriate pocket.

6. The second player takes his/her turn following the same procedure.

7. A card answered incorrectly is placed at the bottom of the pile to be used again later.

8. When all hearts have been used, the player with the most points is declared the winner.

VARIATIONS

With a change of picture, title, and cards, this idea can be expanded into a number of games.

Use pictures of pigs and title the game, "THIS LITTLE PIG." A game with pictures of sheep can become "LAMB CHOP." "BUNNY HOP" is a good title when pictures of rabbits are used. The title, "SHAMROCK SHUFFLE" is appropriate when the board is sprinkled with shamrocks of various sizes that are cut from green construction paper. Cut the naugahyde pockets in the shape of baskets, cut game cards in the shape of eggs, and the game can become "EGGS IN THE BASKET."

"YOUR STATE" GAME

Make a game board individualized for your state by using a small outline of your state to make the spots on the game trail.

Decorate the board with pictures of your state symbols. Pictures of these are usually available from the state tourism office.

Use a picture of the state capital in the winner's spot and title the game, "REACH THE CAPITAL."

On the game cards, use questions about the history and geography of your state as well as questions about government, economics, famous people, tourist sights.

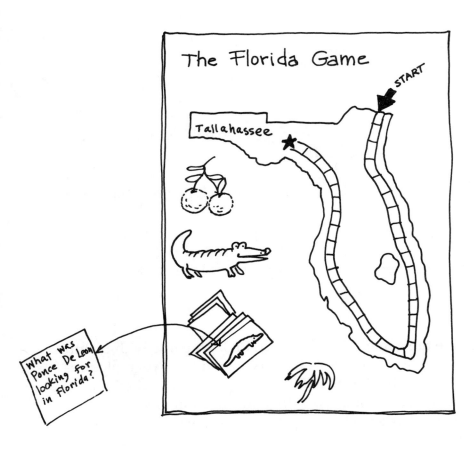

CATCH THE GHOST

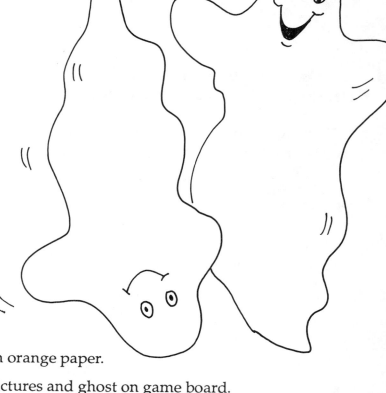

GRADE LEVEL
1-3

PURPOSE
To practice beginning sounds
(consonants, blends).

MATERIALS NEEDED:
- 1 poster board (18" x 22")
- 1 piece orange construction paper
  or gummed art paper
- ghost pattern
- small Halloween pictures (cut from
  workbooks or use patterns given)
- game marker for each player
- index card (5" x 8")

CONSTRUCTION
1. Trace and cut the ghost pattern from orange paper.

2. Leaving room for game title, glue pictures and ghost on game board.

NOTE: If pictures are unavailable, use an opaque projector to enlarge and transfer the illustrated game board to the large poster board.

3. If an answer key will be used, put a small number beside each picture on the game board.

4. Letter game title in upper left corner.

5. With black marker, draw a "squiggle" around each picture. Make black line connections between pictures and to the ghost.

6. Laminate.

7. Use index card to make answer key.

Hint: To avoid cutting twice, don't cut the strips apart until **after laminating**.

7. Laminate all pieces. Cut strip tags apart.

8. Punch two holes along the top edge of each picture card. With X-ACTO® knife, make two slits the same distance apart as holes punched on cards at the top of the witch's apron.

(IMPORTANT: Make holes the same distance apart on each card and make slits on apron of equal distance so that all cards can be fitted to apron interchangeably.)

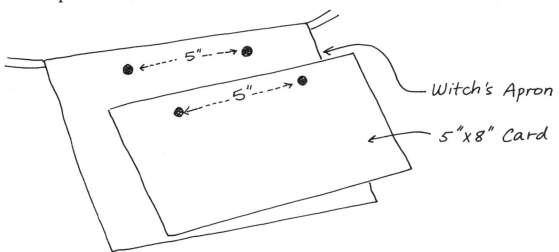

9. From naugahyde, cut two shaped pockets as illustrated on pattern. Staple pockets to shoes.

10. Cover the storage box with self-adhesive paper.

PLAYERS

One – for individual practice
Two – for competition
Small group – under teacher-direction

PROCEDURE

(for two players)

1. Players need pencil and paper for keeping score.

2. With two brads, fasten one of the 5" x 8" picture cards to the witch's apron.

3. Hang the witch on the bulletin board at eye level with two student desks placed facing the witch.

4. Stack appropriate strip tags faceup on one of the student desks.

5. The first player reads the statement on the top card WITHOUT PICKING IT UP and states whether it is fact or opinion. He/she then picks up the strip and checks the back for the correct answer. If he/she has given the proper answer, he/she places the strip tag in the appropriate pocket and records a point for himself/herself.

6. The second player takes a turn following the same procedure.

7. Strip tags not identified correctly can go into a discard stack and may or may not be used again at the end of the round.

8. When all strip tags have been used, the player with the most recorded points is declared the winner.

9. Another round may be played by changing the picture on the witch's apron.

VARIATIONS

To use the board with other skills, staple other labels over the words FACT and OPINION. If no picture is needed, simply leave the witch's apron blank.

By leaving off labels entirely, the game can be used without pencil/paper scorekeeping. Each player uses one of the pockets as his/her own. The player takes a strip tag from the stack and does what is required – define the word, solve the math problem, etc. If a correct answer is given, the player places the strip in his/her pocket. When all strip tags have been used, the player having the most tags in his/her pocket is the winner. Answers may be checked by using the reverse side of the strip tag or with an answer key.

REMINDER: Once again, color-code strip tags of different skills in order to prevent mixups. (All math questions on red tags, vocabulary on blue tags, etc.)

REACH THE STAR

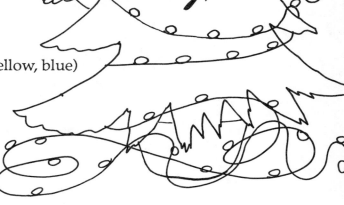

GRADE LEVEL
3-6 depending on cards used

PURPOSE
To review skill or any content. (These instructions are based on review and practice of synonyms and antonyms.)

MATERIALS NEEDED:
- 1 green poster board (22" x 28")
- 1 yellow poster board (6" x 6")
- patterns – tree, star, lights, or ornaments
- gummed art paper (one sheet each of red, yellow, blue)
- 33 game cards
- game marker for each player
- 2 index cards (5" x 8")
- box to hold game pieces
- self-adhesive paper to cover storage box

CONSTRUCTION

1. Use opaque projector to transfer tree pattern on page 110 to fill green poster board. Cut out tree if desired.

2. From art paper, cut thirty-five tree lights (same size as on tree pattern.) Make some of each color. (This game was originally made by cutting tree lights from Christmas wrapping paper.)

3. Position and stick lights on tree. Print "START" on tree light at lower left.

4. Use marker to connect lights with "electric wires."

5. On tree trunk, draw a 2" x 4" rectangle for game cards.

6. Cut star from yellow poster board. Print, "YOU WIN" on the star.

7. Laminate tree and star separately. Glue or staple the star to top of tree.

8. Print game questions or problems on cards. Number each card at upper left and indicate forward movement in lower right corner. (Example: "Move ahead 1.")

9. Print rules and answer key on index cards. Laminate.

10. Cover storage box with self-adhesive paper.

PLAYERS

Two or three players
One judge

PROCEDURE

1. Each player, in turn, draws a card, reads question aloud, and gives answer.

2. Judge reads the correct answer.

3. For a correct answer, player moves forward as indicated on game card and then places card in a discard stack.

4. For an incorrect answer, player does not move. Card goes to the bottom of the stack on the tree trunk.

5. First player to "Reach the Star" is the winner.

VARIATION

Use different game cards to fit this game to any skill, content, or any age group.

Hint: To avoid mixups of game cards, make each stack of cards a different color (synonyms and antonyms, blue; math questions, yellow; science questions, pink; etc.).

SYNONYM AND ANTONYM CARDS TO USE WITH "REACH THE STAR."

- Give a synonym for LOVINGLY.
  Move ahead 2.

- Give an antonym for ASLEEP.
  Move ahead 1.

- Give a sentence using a pair of synonyms.
  (Example: "I feel **sad** and **blue**.)
  Move ahead 3.

- Give a synonym for SMILE.
  Move ahead 1.

- Give a synonym for BABY.
  Move ahead 1.

- Give a synonym for CALLED.
  Move ahead 1.

- Give an antonym for THICK.
  Move ahead 1.

- Fill in the blank with a synonym for the underlined word:

  "The _____ maiden bit into the <u>beautiful</u> apple."
  Move ahead 2.

- Give an antonym for UGLY.
  Move ahead 1.

- Give a synonym for CHILD.
  Move ahead 2.

- Give a sentence using a pair of antonyms.
  Move ahead 3.

- Give a synonym for WALK.
  Move ahead 1.

- Give a synonym for EMPTY.
  Move ahead 1.

- Give an antonym for BEGINNING.
  Move ahead 1.

- Fill in the blank with a synonym for the underlined word:

  "A <u>frightened</u> boy and his _____ friend ran from the dog."
  Move ahead 3.

- Give an antonym for HAPPY.
  Move ahead 1.

- Give a synonym for SMALL.
  Move ahead 1.

- Give an antonym for GOOD.
  Move ahead 1.

- Give an antonym for NIGHT.
  Move ahead 1.

- Give an antonym for TALL.
  Move ahead 1.

- Give an antonym for FOUND.
  Move ahead 1.

- Give a sentence using a pair of antonyms.
  Move ahead 3.

Give a synonym for

LOVINGLY.

Move ahead 2.

- Give a sentence using a pair of synonyms.
  Move ahead 3.

- Fill the blank with an antonym for the underlined word:

  "The <u>tall</u> trees shaded the _____ bushes from the sun."
  Move ahead 2.

- Fill the blank with a synonym for the underlined word:

  "It was a <u>hot</u> day and my skin felt _____."
  Move ahead 2.

- Fill the blank with an antonym for the underlined word:

  "I had to put on a <u>dry</u> shirt after I got _____ in the rain."
  Move ahead 2.

PENALTY AND REWARD CARDS FOR "REACH THE STAR."

1. The Christmas tree fell over. Oh, dear! Go back to START.

2. Oh, you decorated the tree so well! Take 1 extra turn.

3. OOPS! You fell off the ladder trying to put the star on the top of the tree. Rest 1 turn.

4. GOOD FOR YOU! You remembered to put the trunk in wet sand to keep the tree from catching fire. Move ahead 2 spaces.

5. Oh, no! You wouldn't set up the tree? Go back 2.

VARIATION ON "REACH THE STAR" GAME BOARD

Varied ornament shapes can be used instead of the bulb pattern to create the game board. Use the patterns below in the size shown. Affix to the poster tree in a track progression from lower left to treetop. Connect shapes with colored marker lines.

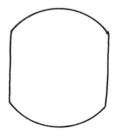 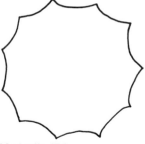 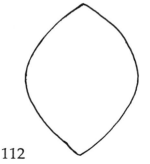 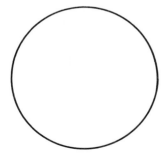

SANTA'S SACKS

GRADE LEVEL
1-6

PURPOSE
To provide a motivational alternative
  to the daily work sheet.

MATERIALS NEEDED:
- 1 white poster board (22" x 28")
- 1 white poster board (9" x 12")
- patterns – Santa, sacks
- green and red construction paper
- index cards (5" x 8")
- 1 brad
- X-ACTO® knife
- large envelope to hold Santa Sacks

10"x13" Naugahyde

Work sheets in pockets

5"x10" Naugahyde

CONSTRUCTION
1. Using an opaque projector, transfer Santa pattern to fill left half of the large white poster board.

2. Color Santa.

3. From green construction paper, cut desired number of sacks (use pattern size as shown on page 116).

   For color-coding, make red sacks for math, blue for social studies, yellow for science, etc.

4. Letter a title in the mouth of each sack.

5. Print directions on the tag of each sack.

6. Number each sack.

7. Print problems, words, etc., on each sack. (See examples on page 117.)

8. On an index card, make an answer key for each sack. (Be sure to number and title each key.)

9. On the 9" x 12" poster, print the rules for this activity.

10. Laminate all pieces.

11. With X-ACTO® knife, make a slit by Santa's thumb so he can "hold" a sack.

12. From red construction paper, cut out and laminate letters to spell out "SANTA'S SACKS" on the bulletin board.

PLAYERS
For use by individual students

PROCEDURE
1. Position "sack of the day" so that tip of sack is in the slit in Santa's thumb. Attach sack to the board with brad at the point where the string joins the tag.

2. Fasten Santa to bulletin board at a height so that it will be eye level with students sitting facing Santa.

3. Arrange and fasten letters, "Santa's Sacks" to board.

4. Fasten the 9" x 12" rules card beside the Santa poster.

5. Give directions to the class as follows:

Two students at a time may use Santa's Sacks. Each sack is a work sheet. When you are ready to do the work sheet, move to the desk in front of Santa and work quietly. Use your own paper and pencil. Follow the directions on the sack's tag.

Each day there will be a new sack. Do the sack during the day when you have time.

When you finish the paper, get the proper answer key from the answer key box and check your paper. At the top of your paper, tell how many you got right and put the paper in your folder.

VARIATION
Use naugahyde to make a Santa Sack large enough to hold a stack of work sheets (one per child). Cut two pieces of naugahyde, one 10" x 13" and one 5" x 10". Fit the smaller piece over the bottom half of the larger piece. Staple the two pieces together at the sides and bottom. Cut the top 2 inches of the larger piece in the shape of the top of a sack. Fasten this "sack pocket" to Santa's hand in place of the green construction paper sack. Place in the pocket thirty like work sheets on some subject. Each student will get a work sheet from the pocket and follow the same procedure.

VARIATION II
To adjust this activity for year-round use, a boy or girl holding a lunch sack could be used. Sacks would be cut from brown construction paper. The activity could be called, "BROWN BAG IT."

SLIT

115

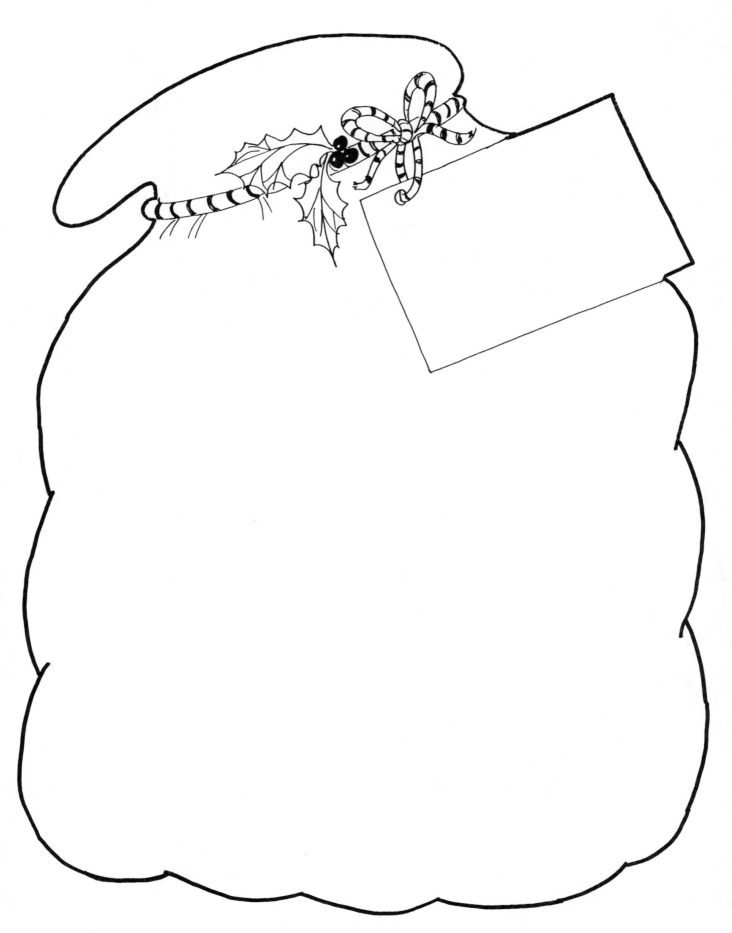

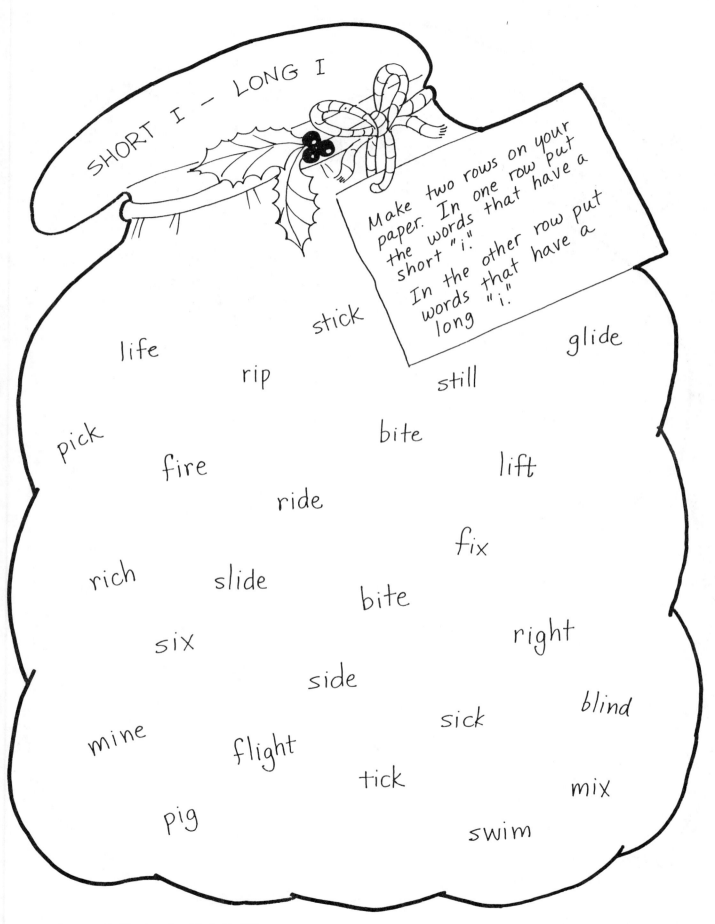

SHORT I — LONG I

Make two rows on your paper. In one row put the words that have a short "i." In the other row put words that have a long "i."

stick

life

rip

still

glide

pick

bite

fire

lift

ride

fix

rich

slide

bite

six

right

side

mine

flight

sick

blind

tick

swim

mix

pig

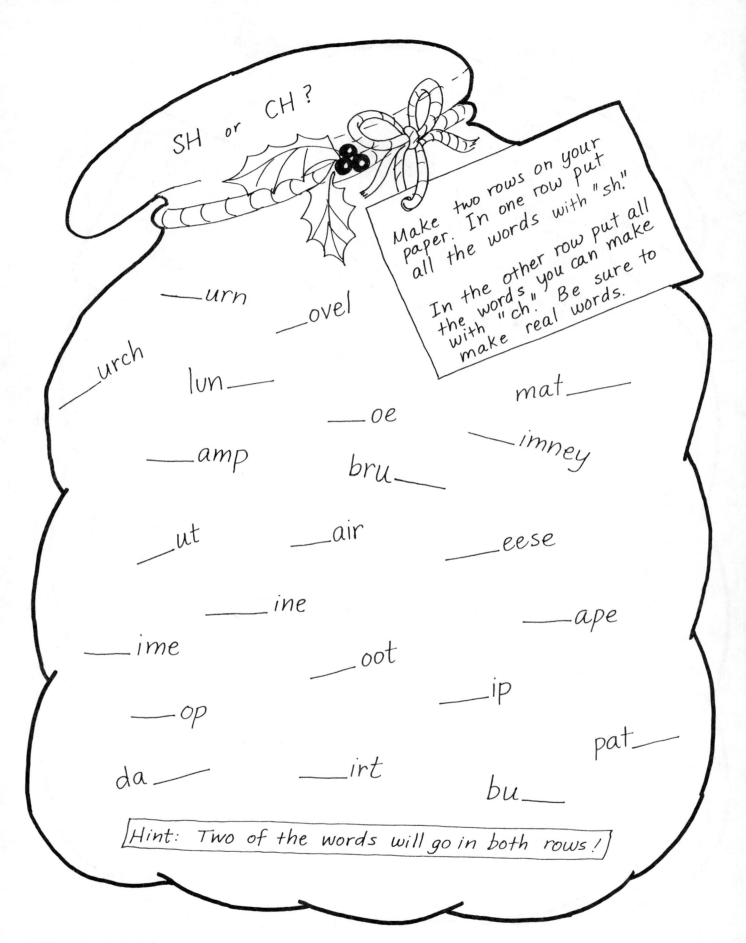

SH or CH?

Make two rows on your paper. In one row put all the words with "sh." In the other row put all the words you can make with "ch." Be sure to make real words.

—urn

_ovel

_urch

lun_

mat_

_oe

_amp

bru_

_imney

_ut

_air

_eese

_ine

_ape

_ime

_oot

_ip

_op

pat_

da_

_irt

bu_

Hint: Two of the words will go in both rows!

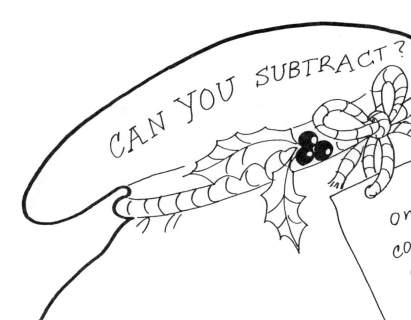

CAN YOU SUBTRACT?

On your paper, copy the problems and fill in the blanks.

1. 15 – 10 = _____
2. 17 – 9 = _____
3. 18 – 9 = _____
4. 10 – 0 = _____
5. 11 – 4 = _____
6. 12 – 5 = _____
7. 13 – 5 = _____
8. 17 – 8 = _____
9. 14 – 4 = _____
10. 13 – 7 = _____

11. 11 – 6 = _____
12. 13 – 8 = _____
13. 12 – 2 = _____
14. 14 – 6 = _____
15. 13 – 4 = _____
16. 15 – 8 = _____
17. 18 – 7 = _____
18. 12 – 3 = _____
19. 10 – 7 = _____
20. 17 – 6 = _____

FRUIT OR VEGETABLE?

Make two rows on your paper. In one row put all the fruits. In the other row put all the vegetables.

onion
banana
apple
carrot
grapes
beans
corn
pear
peas
potatoes

lettuce
orange
strawberry
radish
plum
cucumber
peach
watermelon
tangerine
spinach

SANTA'S SPEECHES

GRADE LEVEL
4-6

PURPOSE
To practice impromptu speaking.

MATERIALS NEEDED:
- index cards (5" x 8")
- Santa patterns
- Christmas stickers (optional)
- box to store Santas
- self-adhesive paper

CONSTRUCTION

1. Make fifteen copies of the Santa face pattern on page 122.

2. Color Santa's hat and nose red, face pink, eyes and mouth black. Decorate one side of the hat with a Christmas sticker if desired.

3. Cut out Santas. Glue each one to a 5" x 8" index card. Cut out an index card following the shape of the Santa face, but leave a 1/4 inch edge of card around the face as illustrated.

NOTE: Gluing the face to the index card will give the face stability, but the 1/4 inch of card overhang is necessary to keep the face and card from separating after lamination.

NOTE II: If you can draw, simply draw the Santa face on an index card or lightweight poster board, color, laminate, and cut out.

4. On each Santa's beard, print a topic for impromptu speaking. (Using red or green ink will give a nice Christmas touch.)

5. Laminate Santa faces.

6. Use self-adhesive paper (a Christmas color perhaps) to cover a storage box for the Santa faces.

PLAYERS
Volunteers or students chosen by the teacher.

PROCEDURE

1. Place all Santas facedown on a table.

2. One student comes forward, picks a Santa, and silently reads the topic.

3. The student should ponder for a minute or two then speak for one minute on the chosen topic.

NOTE: Use topics on one selected day, or starting about two weeks preceding the Christmas holiday, use one card each morning. Use a different student each day.

VARIATION

Make enough topics for each student to have one. Hand out Santas and have students write creatively – stories and/or poems.

To use this activity at a time other than Christmas, make the cutouts in the shape of a telephone, and call the activity "Can We Talk?" Use general topics rather than topics directly related to Christmas.

SUGGESTED TOPICS FOR SANTAS

1. Santa's elves refuse to work anymore and there aren't enough toys ready for Christmas.

2. I made a wonderful snowman. He didn't melt even when the weather got warm.

3. Santa can't find his suit and it's Christmas Eve.

4. The best Christmas gift I ever received.

5. The best Christmas gift I ever gave.

6. Christmas at Grandma's house.

7. How to select a good Christmas tree.

8. Mrs. Santa Claus should...

9. How to decorate a Christmas tree.

10. It is Christmas Eve and Rudolph has run away.

11. How to dress up like Santa Claus.

12. What Christmas smells like.

13. My first Christmas on Mars.

14. When an extraterrestrial came to my house for Christmas.

15. There is something wrong with Rudolph's nose. It won't glow.

TRACKING SANTA

GRADE LEVEL
1-6 depending on cards used

PURPOSE
To practice and/or review any skill or content.

MATERIALS NEEDED:
- 1 white poster board (18" x 22")
- gummed art paper
- scrap poster board cut into game cards (2" x 4")
- 2 index cards (5" x 8")
- game board pattern
- game marker for each player
- small storage box
- self-adhesive paper to cover storage box

CONSTRUCTION

1. Using an opaque projector, transfer the game board pattern to fill the white poster board.

2. Color Santa and the North Pole. Color footprints if desired.

3. Draw in a 2" x 4" rectangle for the game cards.

4. On the game cards, put words to be identified in some way. Math problems may be used. Pictures may be used for younger children.

5. On several of the game cards, print penalties and rewards to be shuffled among the question cards.

6. Number each game card in the upper left corner if an answer key will be used.

7. In the lower right corner of each game card, in small print letter words, "Move Ahead 1," or 2, or 3 depending on the difficulty of the question. (See discussion of game card construction on pages 25-27.)

NOTE: It is not necessary to number or to indicate forward movement on the penalty/reward cards. (See pages 29-30 for penalty/reward cards description.)

8. On index cards, make an answer key and a rules card.

9. Laminate all game pieces.

SUGGESTED PENALTIES AND REWARDS

1. Lost in a terrible snowstorm! Go back 4 spaces.
2. The snow is getting deeper! Stop to put on snowshoes. Lose 1 turn.
3. Lost again? Go back 1 space.
4. A friendly woodcutter showed you the way. Move ahead 1.
5. You're on the right track. Move ahead 2.
6. The North Pole is just ahead. Go 1 more space.
7. You lost your backpack and all your supplies? Go back 3 spaces.

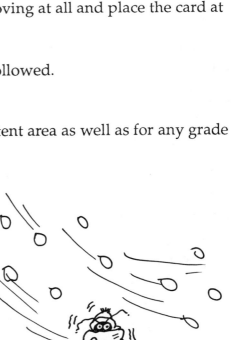

NOTE: Penalty/reward cards should be simplified for younger children.

PLAYERS

Two players and one judge.

PROCEDURE

1. Each player, in turn, draws a card, reads aloud the number on the card, reads aloud the word or problem, and gives an answer.
2. The judge reads the correct answer from the key.
3. A correct answer allows the player to move ahead the number of spaces indicated in the lower right corner of the card.
4. The correctly answered card is placed in a discard stack.
5. For an incorrect answer, the player must remain in place not moving at all and place the card at the bottom of the stack to be answered later.
6. The winner is the first player to reach Santa.
7. When penalty/reward cards are drawn, instructions must be followed.

VARIATION

A change of cards makes this game suitable for any skill or content area as well as for any grade level.

Hint: To avoid mixups, make each different stack of game cards a different color. (Math, red; vocabulary, green, etc.)

To use this game at a time other than Christmas, change the picture and the title. For example, use a brightly colored picture of Mickey Mouse instead of Santa and call the game, "TRACKING MICKEY." Better yet, glue a picture of yourself on the game and call it, "TRACKING MRS./MR. _____." (The kids will love it!)

125

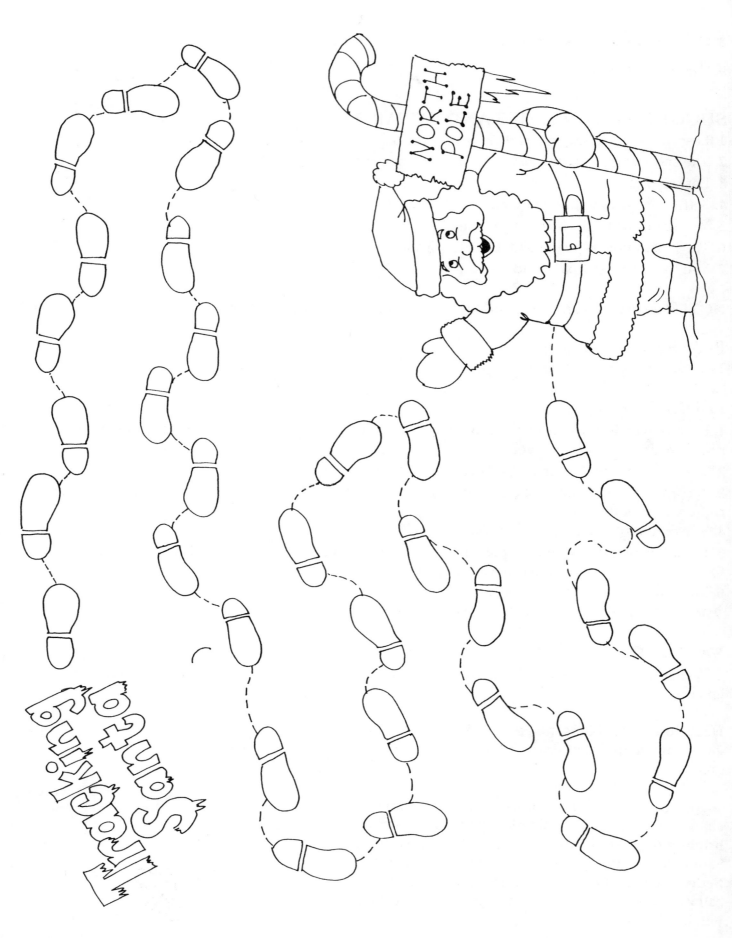